*The World as Event*

Charles Tomlinson

# The World as Event

## The Poetry of Charles Tomlinson

BRIAN JOHN

McGill-Queen's University Press
Montreal and Kingston, London, Buffalo

© McGill-Queen's University Press 1989
ISBN 0-7735-0720-5

Legal deposit fourth quarter 1989
Bibliothèque nationale du Québec

Printed in Canada on acid-free paper

This book has been published with the help of a
grant from the Canadian Federation for the
Humanities, using funds provided by the Social
Sciences and Humanities Research Council of
Canada.

---

**Canadian Cataloguing in Publication Data**

John, Brian, 1935–
    The world as event

    Includes index.
    Bibliography: p.
    ISBN O-7735-0720-5

    1. Tomlinson, Charles, 1927–   --Criticism and
interpretation.   I. Title.

PR6039.0349Z75 1989   8219.914   C89-090158-9

---

*For Margaret*

# Contents

# Acknowledgments

Grateful acknowledgment is made to the following for permission to quote from copyright material:

To Anvil Press Poetry Ltd, for Octavio Paz and Charles Tomlinson, *Airborn/Hijos del Aire* (© Octavio Paz and Charles Tomlinson 1981).

To Oxford University Press, for Charles Tomlinson, *Castilian Ilexes: Versions from Antonio Machado, 1875–1939*, with Henry Gifford (© Oxford University Press 1963); for Charles Tomlinson, *Collected Poems* (© Charles Tomlinson 1985); for Charles Tomlinson, *The Necklace* (1955; reissued 1966; © Oxford University Press 1966); for Charles Tomlinson, *Notes from New York* (© Charles Tomlinson 1984); and for Charles Tomlinson, *The Return* (© Charles Tomlinson 1987).

To Penguin Books Ltd, for permission to quote from *William Carlos Williams: A Critical Anthology*, edited by Charles Tomlinson (Penguin Books 1972; introduction, notes, and selection © Charles Tomlinson 1972).

To Alfred A. Knopf, Inc., and Faber and Faber Ltd, for *The Collected Poems of Wallace Stevens* (© 1954 by Wallace Stevens. All rights reserved).

I wish also to offer my sincere thanks to McMaster University for a research leave; to the Canadian Federation of the Humanities for its grant towards publication; to Darrell Laird for his helpful reading of the manuscript; to Dr Bruce Meyer for his photograph of the poet; to Philip Cercone, Joan McGilvray, and Judith Williams for their advice and editing; and, lastly, to my wife, Margaret, for her constant support and encouragement.

# Abbreviations

All citations for Tomlinson are to the following works and abbreviated thus:

A    *Airborn/Hijos del Aire*, with Octavio Paz (London: Anvil Press Poetry 1981)

America West
South West    *America West South West* (np: San Marcos Press 1970)

BW    *In Black and White: The Graphics of Charles Tomlinson*, intro. Octavio Paz (Cheadle: Carcanet 1976)

CI    *Castilian Ilexes: Versions from Antonio Machado, 1875–1939*, with Henry Gifford (London: Oxford University Press 1963)

CP    *Collected Poems* (Oxford: Oxford University Press 1985)

Eden    *Eden: Graphics and Poetry* (Bristol: Redcliffe Poetry 1986)

N    *The Necklace* (1955; London: Oxford University Press 1966)

NNY    *Notes from New York* (Oxford: Oxford University Press 1984)

PM    *Poetry and Metamorphosis* (Cambridge: Cambridge University Press 1983)

Renga    *Renga: A Chain of Poems*, with Octavio Paz, Jacques Roubaud, and Edoardo Sanguineti,

*The World as Event*

# Introduction

When asked in 1962 whether it was a good or bad period for writing poetry, Robert Graves replied, not unreasonably, "there's nothing wrong with the period, but where are the poets?"[1] Graves's query has since lost much of its pertinence; the map of poetry has changed considerably over the past twenty-seven years, to reveal major accomplishment where only minor talent was suspected, and to refute Theodor Adorno's famous dictum, "No poetry after Auschwitz."[2]

Since the death of Dylan Thomas in 1953, the direction of British poetry has been influenced largely by two wholly contrasting poets, Philip Larkin and Ted Hughes, each of whom has attracted partisan admirers and imitators and by this time has been granted deserved prominence in the mainstream of the English poetic tradition. The one became supreme exemplar for the emerging poetry of the 1950s, its anti-Romantic manifesto proclaimed in Robert Conquest's *New Lines* (1956) and given journalistic baptism as the Movement. The other has inherited a Romanticism derived more particularly from D.H. Lawrence than from Dylan Thomas and the Apocalyptics of the forties, and, despite persistent critical condemnation by some for promoting violence, blood-mystique, and anti-intellectualism, has more recently been appointed Poet Laureate.

The map of poetry, however, is not in fact so neatly divisible; the reality is less tidy and comprehensible. Other major poets whose achievement falls outside such divisions of popular critical history have been at work over the past three decades – not just older established poets like Robert Graves or W.H. Auden but those whose reputations were made since the mid-fifties, above all Geoffrey Hill and R.S.

Thomas. And, if one's scope extended beyond British to Irish poetry over the same period, Thomas Kinsella, John Montague, and Seamus Heaney figure prominently, worthy of comparison with their major British contemporaries. All warrant and in most cases have attracted extended critical attention.

Many such poets have had their imitators and have, in a fashion more European than British, formed groups and issued manifestos. Charles Tomlinson, on the other hand, has remained in relative isolation, remote from the various groups or movements; he has not been widely imitated or had the same impact upon contemporary British poetry as have Larkin and Hughes. Instead, he has sought enrichment from foreign literatures – French, Russian, Spanish, and especially twentieth-century American poetry – and his first substantial volume, *Seeing Is Believing* (1958), was originally published in the United States. Regarded consequently in Britain with varying degrees of suspicion, even distaste, he established early in his career a more considerable reputation abroad: "an Englishman first discovered by the Americans," as one foreign critic has put it.[3]

Yet Tomlinson is, unquestionably in my judgment, among the major contemporary British poets and, with his *Collected Poems* (1985) and his twelfth book of poems, *The Return* (1987), has provided an impressive body of work worthy of sustained critical study. It is still the transatlantic critic who finds it easier to declare him "the most considerable British poet to have made his way since the Second World War."[4] Donald Davie, fellow poet, Tomlinson's Cambridge tutor and longtime friend and admirer, has been less sanguine: "the underrating and misunderstanding of Tomlinson are scandals of such long standing that, when I think of them, I despair."[5] A more accurate estimate of Tomlinson's current reputation probably lies somewhere between these two views. What is less debatable is his significance in any account of contemporary British poetry, both for his own sake and for his status as a kind of test case of British critical sensibility.

If Tomlinson's struggle for acceptance has been both longer and more acrimonious than that of either Larkin or Hughes, one reason may be sought in the supposedly un-English quality of his work, a quality, it must be said, now less susceptible to doubt than at the outset of his career. The charge of being un-English has been made over the centuries against various directions in poetry which are regarded as undesirable, and is based on a peculiarly narrow and static conception of the English poetic tradition. Just as Keats and, in his early years, Tennyson were accused of working outside the English tradition, so too Tomlinson has suffered from such exclusion, and often for the same reasons. His attention to the sensuous, the colourful, sometimes the elegant or epicurean, was regarded in the late fifties and early sixties – in the heyday of the Movement – as dangerously foreign to the moral English line.[6] Keats and Tennyson, both labelled by their contemporary critics as cockney Italianate, hedonistic and unmanly, were likewise seen as preaching an aestheticism remote from and indifferent towards the social and ethical problems of the early nineteenth century, setting art and life in some artificial, decadent, and élitist antithesis. Similar objections were raised at the outset against Tomlinson's work and, indeed, remain in one form or another. He has been credited, somewhat condescendingly, as having pictorial ability – indeed, he trained originally as a painter and in recent years has had numerous exhibitions – capable of recreating landscapes with commendable accuracy and precision, but failing in the last resort to make contact with people.[7] His aesthetic principles – even the very possession of aesthetic principles, it would seem – were thought to create an irrevocable division between the poet and his fellow man and to be applicable at best only to landscapes, physical objects, or private perceptions. Supposedly remote from the business of living, Tomlinson, an academic by profession, was thus placed in the inevitable Ivory Tower and characterized as "donnish"[8] or mandarin or "cerebral."[9] Similarly, remote from everyday English culture, Tomlinson, long-standing supporter of William Carlos Williams and Marianne Moore, translator of Tyutchev, Machado, Vallejo, Ungaretti, and others, proponent of Black Mountain poetics, writer of collective poetry, thus effectively cut himself off from the Hardy mainstream and chose the foreign, American, and essentially modernist sideline, which in Britain of late has been severely discredited, although not wholly dismantled. And while he himself has insisted, "the fundamental interests of a poet's work do not alter,"[10] he has also been charged with lack of development.

These constitute some of the "misunderstandings" of Tomlinson's work of which Davie has despaired, and the problems they raise strike at the heart of English poetry over the last three decades. They may also account for Davie's early emphasis, in his introduction to *The Necklace* (1955), upon the poet's rejection of Romanticism, whether hedonism or Art-for-Art's Sake: "Tomlinson's morality is sternly traditional, classical, almost Augustan" (*N* xvi). Candour, strictness, impartiality, and civility are indeed recurrent value terms in his work, but Tomlinson himself has commented further: "it is an Augustanism that has felt the impact of French poetry – Baudelaire to Valéry – and of modern American poetry."[11] On a previous occasion he argued along similar lines, complaining of the wilful parochialism of his English contemporaries, and particularly in the work of Philip Larkin:

the thing about American poets is that they realize that they have simply got to read the poetry of other languages, they have simply got to read French poetry, whereas so many English poets are so pleased with the parish pump it doesn't seem to concern them that they ought to know what happened in French Symbolism from, say, 1870 to round about 1920: from Rimbaud up to Valéry. All that phase interests me immensely, and I think it has obviously fed the American poets as well, whereas writers of my own generation were not, I think, as poets, particularly interested in that kind of thing. If you go to the works of someone like Larkin you don't touch that level at all.[12]

Indeed, Davie's emphasis upon Tomlinson's near-Augustan morality serves as a useful antidote to the more common early misunderstanding of his American associations, when critics regarded Tomlinson's poetry either as "pastiche" (Elizabeth Jennings, 1960) or as "fighting against the genius of the time and the language" (Philip Hobsbaum, 1965).[13] It is a measure not only of Tomlinson's increased stature over the last fifteen years but of the change in British critical sensibilities that his so-called American qualities and debts are no longer regarded with such dismay or dismissed out of hand as alien, formless, or irrelevant.

Wherever he has sought enrichment of his art, however, Tomlinson has remained intrinsically an English poet, intent upon reawakening English sensibilities to the real nature of the world. "I write as an Englishman who has responded to other horizons," he declared in 1987, "internationally minded, though with the ballast of England and English to keep him – Wordsworth's favourite word – steady."[14] Indeed Tomlinson's internationalism has often obscured his origins in English Romanticism and the lasting influence of Wordsworth. On an earlier occasion he pointed to concerns shared by English Romanticism and American modernism:

Critics have sometimes related my own work to the American poets, and this is just. But the American poets, too, have been concerned, in twentieth-century conditions, with an undertaking that began with the partnership of Wordsworth and Coleridge and their exploration of how the self arrives at knowledge and identity, and of how mind and senses contribute to this process.[15]

Elsewhere Tomlinson provided further indication of his literary ancestry: "A phenomenological poetry, with roots in Wordsworth and in Ruskin, is what I take myself to be writing."[16] While his basic preoccupations have remained essentially unchanged since the first volumes, his vision, like his technical skill, has become increasingly assured, gaining in strength and validity, until it is one of the most compelling, certainly one of the most distinctive and original, in our time.

Charles Tomlinson was born in 1927 at Stoke-on-Trent in the English Midlands, read English at Cambridge and worked in London and Italy before moving to the University of Bristol, where he is now Professor of English Literature. He has travelled widely in Europe, the United States, and Mexico and has translated from several languages. He has published separate editions of his translations of Tyutchev, Machado, and Vallejo, together with a selection of others as *Translations* (1983); is editor of *The Oxford Book of Verse in English Translation* (1980); and has written in quadrilingual collaboration with Octavio Paz, Jacques Roubaud, and Edoardo Sanguineti (*Renga*, 1971) and, with Paz again, produced a bilingual sequence, *Airborn/Hijos del Aire* (1981). He has served as visiting professor at several universities in the United States; written in *Some Americans* (1981) of his contact through various writers and artists with American modernism; while the Clark Lectures he gave at Cambridge in 1982 have been published as *Poetry and Metamorphosis* (1983). He began publishing his own poetry in 1951, with *Relations and Contraries*, and is the author of eleven subsequent volumes, the most recent being *The Return* (1987). In 1985 he brought out his *Collected Poems*. Trained as a painter, he has also exhibited his own graphics on numerous occasions, a selection of his work appearing in *In Black and White* (1975) and *Eden* (1986). He is an Honorary Fellow of Queen's College, Cambridge, and a Fellow of the Royal Society of Literature.

# CHAPTER ONE

# The Language of Sense

From the outset, one of Tomlinson's essential concerns has been to trace the contours and dynamics of the mind in the act of perception. Like Blake, an early influence,[1] he wants to enlighten us about the nature of the self and the world, the interior and exterior landscapes which must remain interrelated if a true and fruitful awareness is to develop. Inheriting from the Romantics, then, their description of that perception as organic, dynamic, and creative, Tomlinson seeks to make clear the interchange or relation which is established between the perceiving self and the object perceived. His poetry has thus been descriptive but, more accurately, epistemological in nature: more than simply capturing an object or a landscape or an experience, it seeks to chart the "exchange" which occurs in perception and particularly in that perception we might call real or whole or true.[2] That is, Tomlinson's poetry turns in upon itself, not out of any narcissism or preferred solipsism – both of which he finds distasteful and negative – but out of an awareness of the self as matrix in our knowledge of the world. "The mind is a hunter of forms," as he affirms on two occasions (CP 189, 233), "binding itself, in a world that must decay, to present substance."

The recurrent critical objections – that Tomlinson's work has little to do with people and that he retreats from contact to the pastoral of a landscape – are thus fundamentally misconceived. His work centres upon how a person sees and makes contact. The bias may be epistemological but the scope is eventually moral, the tone contemplative, the vision near-religious. Furthermore, the poetry turns out upon the world, again because Tomlinson recognizes not only the contribution the subject makes to the object perceived but, with a Wordsworthian sense of reverberation or echo, the effect the world has upon the self. His landscapes are thus never ends in themselves, for all the detailed accuracy and precision of his descriptions. The act of perception as it embraces both self and object is a more central concern, because a proper awareness of the mind's movements and the world's participation in that process can enlighten and illuminate, bring both succour and delight, strength and purpose. "Sensation," in Tomlinson's own words, "... isn't just the naked objects but already a grasping for significance." Again, "in our trusting in the language of the senses we are constructing our selves." Consequently, "for me, the moment of sensation, the taking hold on the physical moment, the meeting of person and presence, are what comes first in my poetry."[3]

In 1975 Octavio Paz, the distinguished Mexican poet, friend and collaborator of Tomlinson, described the process thus:

When I first read one of Charles Tomlinson's poems, over ten years ago, I was struck by the powerful presence of an element which, later, I found in almost all his creative work, even in the most reflective and self-contemplating: the outer world, a presence at once constant and invisible. It is everywhere but we do not see it. If Tomlinson is a poet for whom "the outer world exists," it must be added that it does not exist for him as an independent reality, apart from us. In his poems the distinction between subject and object is attenuated until it becomes, rather than a frontier, a zone of interpenetration, giving precedence not to the subject but rather to the object: the world is not a representation of the subject – rather, the subject is the projection of the world. In his poems, outer reality – more than merely the space in which our actions, thoughts and emotions unfold – is a climate which involves us, an impalpable substance, at once physical and mental, which we penetrate and which penetrates us. The world turns to air, temperature, sensation, thought; and we become stone, window, orange peel, turf, oil stain, helix.

Against the idea of the world-as-spectacle, Tomlinson opposes the concept – a very English one – of the world as event. (BW 7)

Moreover, Tomlinson himself has talked of the moral nature of his landscapes,[4] and already any Keatsian indulgence of the senses seems remarkably misplaced. Nevertheless, particularly in his early volumes, the poet reveals an opulence and epicureanism directly traceable to another and more influential master, the American poet Wallace Stevens. Tomlinson has admitted to being "haunted" in his early years by Stevens: "It was a case of being haunted rather than of cold imitation. I was also a painter and this meant that I had far more interest in the particulars of a landscape or an object than Stevens. Stevens rarely makes one *see* anything in detail for all his talk about a physical universe."[5] Likewise, in his Author's Preface to the 1966 reprinting of *The Necklace*, Tomlinson acknowledged his debt in terms which refute charges of idolatry and pastiche: "the poems were both a dialogue with and a departure from him." "Stevens's sense of the complex relation of observer and environment fascinated me, but was there ever a poetry which stood so explicitly by a physical universe and against transcendence, but which gives so little account of that universe, its spaces, patterns, textures, 'a world of canon and fugue,' such as Hopkins spoke of seeing before him?"[6]

Not only discontented by Stevens's inadequate treatment of the physical world, Tomlinson objected also to his insistence upon "the supreme fiction," that extreme Berkeleyan subjectivism in which the very existence of the world depends upon the perceiving self. Instead, Tomlinson insists upon "according objects their own existence" (Author's Preface, *N*), or what in his later work he describes as the "otherness" of things. Hence, in the first poem of his bilingual sonnet sequence written in conjunction with Octavio Paz, Tomlinson describes their poetry thus:

> Coming to terms with day – light, water, stone –
> our words extend a world of objects
> that remains itself: the new leaves
> gladden us, but for no motive of their own – (*A* 23)

For words do "extend" our knowledge of the world and such knowledge involves the self's participation in an organic exchange, a "Coming to terms" which suggests both negotiation and articulation. Yet the world "remains itself" and the tree's new foliage, for all its gladdening effect upon the perceiving selves, fulfils its own identity and function. While in an early poem, "The Mediterranean," he affirms "The imagination cannot lie" (*CP* 21), he rejects the extremity of Stevens's position just as he rejects Keats's also; the world's externality is set against the despotic authority of the Stevensian creative self and against the total abnegation of the Keatsian Negative Capability. Rather, the exchange Tomlinson seeks between self and world honours the individuality of each, a position closer to both Wordsworth and D.H. Lawrence than to either of his previous models. He is aware "that when the truth is not good enough / We exaggerate." But, in opposing exaggeration, he proceeds in the same poem to assert also that

### Proportions

Matter. It is difficult to get them right.
There must be nothing
Superfluous, nothing which is not elegant
And nothing which is if it is merely that.   ("The Art of Poetry," 11)

The violence of the enjambement – in this case between stanzas and heightened by the immediately impeding period – places extraordinary emphasis upon the word "Matter." For not only do proportions "matter" (signify, be important) but also they have considerable bearing upon the element of matter, the physical substance which we understand more completely through recognition of proportions as opposed to exaggeration.

The Stevensian elegance thus unbalances and exaggerates; proportion, on the other hand, is crucial, whether to self or senses. Equally, in another early poem, "Observation of Facts" (11–12), he firmly dismisses pure objectivity: "Facts have no eyes." In order to go beyond mere fact to the essential *quidditas* of a thing, one needs to regard "Facets of copiousness." The term "copiousness" disappears from Tomlinson's work after 1958 ("The Jam Trap," 33) but resurfaces in the "Copious tree" in a quatrain contributed by Octavio Paz to the collaborative sonnet sequence, *Airborn*, previously quoted. Such "copiousness" suggests the "rotundity" or "fatness" which Stevens consistently promoted:[7] his "rotund emotions" are those which are capable of containing or embracing more of the world and so enlarging the perceiving self. For Tomlinson, however, such copiousness is possible only "when we have silenced ourselves" (12) and achieved the proper degree of detachment in our relationship with the world. It is not that he wishes to deny the contribution of the creative self in the act of perception; rather, he seeks to reinstate the externality of the world, which Stevens's supremely fictive self tended to undervalue or exclude. The argument is extended in "Observation of Facts," to both mythology and elegance, as to any other "curtain" hindering our contact with the world's otherness or that which is "bodied over against one":[8]

A dryad is a sort of chintz curtain
Between myself and a tree.
The tree stands: or does not stand:
As I draw, or remove the curtain.

The house encloses: or fails to signify
As being bodied over against one,
As something one has to do with.

The room flowers once one has introduced
Mental fibre beneath its elegance,
A rough pot or two, outweighing
The persistence of frippery
In lampshades or wallpaper. (11–12)

There is thus an imaginative exchange of selves which takes place between subject and object, perceiver and world, and which is possible only if elegance is kept under control, if the proper balance of impersonality and creativity of self is maintained, and if the individual existence of both self and world is honoured:

the particular, rather than existing in its own isolate intensity, means first of all the demands of a relationship – you are forced to look, feel, find words for something not yourself – and it means, like all relationships, a certain forgetfulness of self, so that in contemplating something, you are drawn out of yourself towards that and towards other people – other people, because though the words you use are *your* words, they are also *their* words: you are learning about the world by using the common inheritance of language. And once you are moving on into your poem, rather than "isolate intensity," you are aware of belonging among objects and among human beings and it is a great stay for the mind, this awareness. And a great chastener in that you realize that you in your *own* isolate intensity would be an egotist and a bore.[9]

Like Wordsworth,[10] Tomlinson seeks to achieve a balance between the two extreme positions – whether of self or world – and only in the last decade has redirected readers to his relationship to "Wordsworth and Coleridge, whose memory and example underlie much of what I have written. Both of them speak the language of sense, or of sensation (perception, as we should say), and they are the first poets to be deeply aware of the way our trusting to the language of sense – the way that perception is primary to all our notions – binds together and builds the human self."[11] Like Wordsworth again, as well as Keats and Stevens, Tomlinson is equally aware of the necessary reverberation which occurs in perception, a "wedding of the mind," as he calls it:

> There are two
> ways to marry with a land –
> first, this bland and blind
> submergence of the self, an act
> of kind and questionless. The other
> is the thing I mean, a whole
> event, a happening, the sound
> that brings all space in
> for its bound, when self is clear
> as what we keenest see and hear:
> no absolute of eye can tell
> the utmost, but the glance
> goes shafted from us like a well.   ("How it happened,"77–8)

Tomlinson seeks not "submergence of the self," which is both "bland and blind," but "a whole / event, a happening" in which keenness of self and of senses are interdependent and lead to an experience of the dynamic whole. He rejects any absolutism of the eye, as elsewhere he rejects Romantic transcendence, preferring "the glance" which, with its imagery of "shaft" and "well," unites searching keenness with the movement of "event" and penetration into the core of things. The eye image is as central to Tomlinson's purpose as to that of another contemporary British poet, Ted Hughes. Both poets strive to express an inclusiveness of vision – what Tomlinson in "Portrait in Stone" (94) calls a "matrimony" which "Makes mind and eye unanimous." Where Hughes, however, emphasizes the wide-eyed perception and muscularly dynamic experience of his animals, Tomlinson is inclined to stress keenness of sight – hence his value terms of clarity, lucidity, acuity, discrimination – possessing a more rational and intellectual character than the physicality of vision associated with Hughes. The difference is evident in those Tomlinson poems where he seems almost to be challenging Hughes on his own ground and produces a markedly different and original poem – "The Atlantic" (17), "Crow" (68–9), "The Fox," "Bone," "Wind" (109–11), "Hawks" (215), "The Faring," "Macduff," and "The Scream" (291, 307–8, 309–10). Like Hughes, he can reject mere factual knowledge or abstraction as providing only half-truths, but shows little inclination to pursue Hughes's subterranean paths into darkness. "Visual art," as Tomlinson has defined it, is "not an unleasher of the 'subconscious', but a cure for blindness" (BW 22). Yet our eyes too can deceive us and be deceived in turn: "our eyes (our lies)" (CP 217). Instead, the eye must be informed by the other senses – a process which in "Château de Muzot" (46) he describes as one where "the eye / Tactually commends" – and so become "a single, judicious eye."[12]

That light which seemed
to have drawn out after it
all space, melting in horizontals,
must yield now
to a new, tall beam,
a single, judicious eye:   ("Nocturnal," 119)

Tomlinson's image describes nocturnal moonlight replacing the declining sun, telling "in its own style / this tale of confusions," its judiciousness of eye reflecting that character of self the poet approves of and practises.

Just as the eye must relate to the mind and the other four senses, so too must the imaginative self relate to the external world, in a "marriage" or "wedding" or, to use another recurrent image, a "truce." In an act of creative perception the judicious eye negotiates between the perceiver and the perceived, as if a frontier (yet another image) existed, requiring diplomacy and tact.[13] Sometimes the spanning of subject and object is expressed by way of a bridge ("Eden," 159; "Against Extremity," 163) and, with the example of Hart Crane and more particularly Marianne Moore before him, Tomlinson can be drawn to Brooklyn Bridge (as in the early "Over Brooklyn Bridge" in American Scenes or in the more recent volume, Notes from New York). For bridges, like truces, involve tact or touch, unite that which is separated, and permit exchanges and communication. Consequently, in a prose poem in *The Way of a World* Tomlinson captures a particular moment as daylight ends, the moment in which the exchange negotiated highlights the individuality of both subject and object, and enables the perceiver to "measure" himself, both the actual present and the hoped-for future, against the "demands" of the external world. The poem is a further elaboration of the eye's judicious character and constitutes another "nocturne." Its very structure, moving from anatomical statement through precise perception to repetition of opening phrasing, contributes to the considerable sense of completion and truce.

The muscles which move the eyeballs, we are told, derive from a musculature which once occupied the body end to end ... Sunblaze as day goes, and the light blots back the scene to iris the half-shut lashes. A look can no longer extricate the centre of the skyline copse. But the last greys, the departing glows caught by the creepers bearding its mass, prevail on the half-blinded retina. Branches deal with the air, vibrating the beams that thread into one's eye. So that "over there" and "in here" compound a truce neither signed – a truce that, insensibly and categorically, grows to a decree, and what one hoped for and what one is, must measure themselves against those demands which the eye receives, delivering its writ on us through a musculature which occupies the body end to end.

("Poem," 192)

The imagery, like the principle, recurs throughout Tomlinson's work: in "Black Nude" (93) the poet sees that "White architectured distances / Ride sleeping in the clear truce of her eye" – the image resurfaces in *The Return* (1987) as an aural "truce" of air and water (34); the first section of *American Scenes* is entitled "Negotiations"; while in *The Way In* he still refers to "light's guarded frontier" ("In March," *CP* 255) or, in a sincerely felt poem, "After a Death" (253–4), seeks for meaning along that frontier to understand a person's death:

> That space
> Drawing the eye up to its sudden frontier
>   Asks for a sense to read the whole
> Reverted side of things.

In the prose poem above, Tomlinson used another image, inherited from Donne, of beams "threading" into one's eyes.[14] The image captures nicely that weaving interpenetration which he elsewhere describes as "meshing" or like a "skein," imagery present from the beginning. Hence, in *Written on Water* he writes of the Ariadne legend ("Ariadne and the Minotaur," 213); continues to follow the "thread / Through the labyrinth of appearances" in the title poem (236); while later, in *The Way In*, he pursues the "thread of song" (270). Even Tomlinson's development of the three-ply line, learnt from William Carlos Williams[15] and Marianne Moore, suitably emulates the unravelling of an experience, the cadence of a visual or an intellectual perception, while at the same time capturing the rhythms and inflections of the speaking voice. In Tomlinson's own words, "language stylizes our perception"; hence, of Williams's famous wheelbarrow poem, he proceeds to insist upon the essential unity of form and meaning: "It's the form of language – the speed of meditation through written language *depends* on the wheelbarrow."[16] The thread and related imagery are more obviously visual expressions of Tomlinson's attempt to capture the dynamic and labyrinthine nature of experience. An equally dominant image working towards the same end, however, is that of music, inherited from Stevens and the French Symbolists.

A perception never occurs in a vacuum; the self experiencing that perception is able, through analysis and memory, to establish associations among particular perceptions. The creative self thus becomes proficient at placing perceptions within an ever-increasing context, recognizing similarities and distinctions, and so enriching and defining the experience, making it more real and more completely known. The influence of French Symbolism, with its intrinsic faith in art's aspiration to the condition of music, led Tomlinson early to see a complex musical patterning within the self's experiences. His own practice as a poet and painter points to a similarly Symbolist alliance of the arts. Indeed, he has even had poems set to music and exhibited his own paintings and graphics. His models, influences, and examples have been sought in both music and painting as well as literature. Vermeer, Constable, Ruskin, Millet, Thomas Eakins, Cézanne, Van Gogh, Magritte, Braque – all play their part in the poetry, as do Mozart, Beethoven, Schumann, Schoenberg, and Brückner. Ruskin particularly has been a seminal influence[17] – indeed Tomlinson's prose poems resemble entries in Ruskin's journals – though his "chief interest had always been Cézanne and then in Cubism" while recent influences have been more decidedly surrealist (Oscar Domínguez and Gaudí) (*BW* 121; *Eden* 73). Whatever the period or style, music and the visual arts remain the dominant analogues; the poem, so he has argued, creates "an imaginary space"[18] within which meaning, particularly of a musical kind, is to be sought. "As the mind attends to the pulsation of the growing poem, it is as if it enters and shares this created space which, filled by the invitations of movement and sound, seems at once landscape and music, perhaps more music than landscape." "Rhythm," consequently, "helps the mind to think into unity"; it also joins proportion in the war against Romantic excess, whether of emotion or self.

To handle measure thus seems a human thing to do: your recurrences are never so pat as to seem simply mechanical, your outgrowths never so rambling or brambled as to spread to mere vegetation. A human measure, surrounded by surprises, impenetrable and unknowable, but always reasserting itself, could be a salutary aim – one in which rhythm and tone are allies – faced as we always are by the temptation to exaggerate and to overvalue the claims of self.

In the first volumes the sources of Tomlinson's preoccupation with music are more explicitly French Symbolism and Wallace Stevens. In "Aesthetic," the opening poem of *The Necklace*, for example, he argues that "Reality is to be sought, not in concrete / But in space made articulate" and points to "The sea-voice / Tearing the silence from the silence" (*CP* 3). We are meant to think not only of Mallarmé's "silence" but of the correspondence of sensory qualities by which art aspires to the condition of music. In the exchange between perceiver and perceived there occurs that synaesthetic exchange in which colours, taste, smells, touch, and sounds mingle – that which Rimbaud referred to as "le dérèglement de tous les sens" or Baudelaire as "correspondances." The principle is no longer esoterically Symbolist, as Donald Davie has rightly argued (*N* xii), but part of our more everyday understanding. Hence, among the "Nine Variations in a Chinese Winter Setting," the title itself suggesting also the extent of Stevens's early influence, we are given "variations" or correspondences of sensations. While the poem first appears to be little more than a latter-day exercise in Imagism, Tomlinson handles the technique with considerable dexterity so as to go beyond mere exercise and to capture the essential nature of the experience.

I
Warm flute on the cold snow
Lays amber in sound.

II
Against brushed cymbal
Grounds yellow on green,
Amber on tinkling ice.

III
The sage beneath the waterfall
Numbers the blessing of a flute;
Water lets down
Exploding silk.

IV
The hiss of raffia,
The thin string scraped with the back of the bow
Are not more bat-like
Than the gusty bamboos
Against a flute.

V
Pine-scent
In snow-clearness
Is not more exactly counterpointed
Than the creak of trodden snow
Against a flute. (*CP* 3–4)

"The proliferation of resemblances," as Stevens wrote, "extends an object"; or, again, "Poetry is a satisfying of the desire for resemblance."[19] Yet even towards this basic principle, as epitomized in Stevens's "Thirteen Ways of Looking at a Blackbird," Tomlinson can afford to be irreverent: "one doesn't always want to be wondering how many ways there are of looking at a blackbird. There ought to be times when one way is enough or the existence of *that* blackbird is enough. Consciousness that becomes merely a disease of prying, a bullying assertion of its own dear self, can be not merely obtrusive but comic – I think of some of Proust's more excessive moments."[20]

From the outset, from his pamphlet *Relations and Contraries* (1951), Tomlinson has relied upon the principle and imagery of music to convey the essential character of his experience. His sources and inspiration have constantly been musical also, whether the Mozartian lightness, dexterity, and wit which, from the early *Solo for a Glass Harmonica* (1957), he surely emulates, or Schoenberg's counterpoint, celebrated in a magnificent ode on the violin concerto. Moreover, he can also write the satirical "Beethoven Attends the C Minor Seminar" (*CP* 267-8) or reveal a wry affection for the Falstaffian figure of the double bass ("Consolations for Double Bass," 269). Above all, perhaps, as Donald Davie has argued, is Tomlinson's preference for the flute. His "Three Wagnerian Lyrics" (225-6) satirize Wagnerian excess and are grouped in *Written on Water* with other "bagatelles"; indeed, an early poem, "Flute Music," correlates brass with excess while elevating the flute for its Augustan qualities (rationality, setting limits to passion, and, in its peace, gaining a vision of moderation and justice).

> The glare of brass over a restless bass
> (Red glow across olive twilight)
> Urges to a delighted excess,
> A weeping among broken gods.

> The flute speaks (reason's song
> Riding the ungovernable wave)
> The bound of passion
> Out of the equitable core of peace. (9)

Just as the two terms, ungovernable/equitable, are held in nicely balanced antithesis in the stanza, so too the Yeatsian "ungovernable wave"[21] is mastered finally to create an Augustan equity. Likewise, in "Nine Variations in a Chinese Winter Setting," the flute is seen as defining "the tangible borders of a mood" (4), much as "the single voice" of the violin, in "Chaconne for Unaccompanied Violin" (99), provides "the measure / of a solitude."[22]

Such a vision constitutes the "measure" of things, a term Tomlinson inherits from Stevens and one that is conveniently musical in origin. For "measure" involves encompassment (embracing the world in its rich multifariousness), but also definition and assessment (the setting of limits to passion and cocking a cooler, more detached, objective eye), while at the same time reminding us that clear perceptions will recognize the musical nature of experience. Hence, the superbly accomplished early poem "At Delft: Johannes Vermeer, 1632–75" (32) captures the "measure" of both the moment and the scene. In its subtitle reference, the poem acknowledges Vermeer, who painted two *Views of Delft* and, like Tomlinson, was much preoccupied with interiors, geometry, and light. However, more than acknowledgment of a past master, the poem in turn establishes the moral as well as epistemological character of the Dutch interior genre. As in "Flute Music," we move inside to the centre or core, a movement which recurs with increasing significance in Tomlinson's search for the essences of things. The chiming of the town's clocks is seen to function in a variety of ways: first, it "admits" the day, thus both measuring and conceding time; secondly, it expresses time's musical measure; and, lastly, the clocks' very simultaneousness confers a "civic" quality upon the day. The same civic sense and measure occur in the geometry of the town's plan ("each street / Its neighbour's parallel, each house / A displacement in that mathematic"). The movement inside, however, reminds us that Delft is not merely "a staid but dancing town," and the civic quality the poet has identified is extended to the house interior. There is the same balance of antitheses – coolness and opulence – which brings clarity of perception, wholeness of experience, and the civic nature is repeated in good Symbolist fashion in both exterior and interior, albeit in a change of "key":

Within
The key is changed: the variant recurs
   In the invariable tessellation of washed floors,
As cool as the stuffs are warm, as ordered
   As they are opulent. White earthenware,
A salver, stippled at its lip by light,
   The light itself, diffused and indiscriminate
On face and floor, usher us in,
   The guests of objects: as in a landscape,
All that is human here stands clarified
   By all that accompanies and bounds. The clocks
Chime muted underneath domestic calm.

The poem's own counterpointed lines shape the whole within bounds and into ordered perspective. With nice irony, we are ushered in, "The guests of objects," with proper recognition of all that is external to us and the possession of that necessary civic detachment or "domestic calm" practised in seventeenth-century Delft. "Measure" – or, in some instances, "style" (*The Way In*) or "melody" (*Notes from New York*) – remains a recurrent value term and preoccupation. Whatever the term used, however, the function remains the same – the coming to terms with an experience and capturing its distinctive nature, whether as musical measure or style.

In the early volumes Tomlinson was more easily tempted into a Stevensian exoticism. More so than in his later years, his world is shot through with vivid colours, particularly the predominant Stevens primary colours (green, blue, red), and he can object, after Stevens, to "The white mind" (50). The inclination towards word-music, which Stevens shared with the Nineties and, earlier, Keats and Tennyson, is also present:

Beneath dawn a sardonyx may be cut from it
In white layers laced with a carnelian orange,
A leek- or apple-green chalcedony
Hewn in the cold night.   ("Sea Change," 7)

At times the exotic approaches the Stevensian epicurean, as in "Fiascherino" where the sea frays sticks "to the newly carved / Fresh white of chicken flesh" (12). But such extravagance gives way early to a more judicious response to the world's multifariousness. In "Maillol," for example, he praises the sculptor's awareness of the "bar between / a plenitude and a luxury" (90). The elegant, exotic, and opulent are balanced increasingly against proportion and mass, angle and distance, that draughtsman's preoccupation with perspective which has given rise in Tomlinson to an architectural sense and to peculiarly geometrical imagery. For, like the flute, the geometrical – cube, arc, parallel, axis, centre – sets limits, defines precisely, keeps passion within bounds. Praising "The patient geometry" of the formal landscape in "The Chestnut Avenue" (75), the poet is thus struck by man's imposition of mindful order, like "the civility of the façade" of the house itself, both of which are assailed by the barbarism of the natural world. Consequently, in Octavio Paz's words, "His procedure approaches, at one extreme, science: maximum objectivity and purification, though not suppression, of the subject"; yet "his poems are experiences and not experiments. Aestheticism is an affectation, contortion, preciosity, and in Tomlinson we find rigour, precision, economy, subtlety" (*BW* 8). "Painting is a science," the English painter Constable had likewise asserted previously, "and should be pursued as an inquiry into the laws of nature. Why, then, may not landscape painting be considered as a branch of natural philosophy, of which pictures are but the experiments?" The assertion provides the epigraph to "A Meditation on John Constable" (*CP* 33–5), and while the poet might praise the landscape painter's hand which "Bodied the accurate and total knowledge," he is also certain that "Art / Is complete when it is human" and that "The artist lies / For the improvement of truth."

The danger of such an analogy between science and art and a preoccupation with geometry is the possible reduction to "the impersonality of anatomy" (7), a bodilessness as unacceptable, because unreal, as its opposite, Stevens's élitist opulence. Consequently, in "Through Binoculars," the poet declares,

This fictive extension into madness
Has a kind of bracing effect:
That normality is, after all, desirable
One can no longer doubt having experienced its opposite. (7)

Or, in "The Jam Trap," taking an object normally devoid of aesthetic considerations, he upholds the aesthetic principle that "Sweetness is not satisfaction / Nor was the elation of the pursuit / The measure of its end" (32). Indeed, such sweetness brings inevitable death rather than satisfaction, a drowning of the self. Instead, the supposedly unaesthetic object must be re-viewed, just as the poet is inclined to use everyday clichés – "No more than meets the eye" (38) or "Seeing is Believing" – to establish a central aesthetic principle. When he offers deliberately prosaic statements, however – "Too little / has been said / of the door" (112) – he has, like Wordsworth in his more prosaic moments, been misunderstood and ridiculed.

Although Tomlinson's roots are more Romantic than Augustan, he has continued to compaign against Romantic excess. Indeed, one of his reasons for turning to modern American poetry and to Stevens particularly was to avoid such excess:

When I started writing poetry, I suppose round about 1948, the atmosphere was still dominated by Dylan Thomas, and I think this prevented many poets from finding their own voice and from looking very clearly at the world outside themselves. It was mostly the job of articulating their own subjective feelings in a rather cloudy manner, with a good deal of the Thomas rhetoric laid on. Now, at this time I happened to have read Stevens and Marianne Moore and later I read Williams, and it seemed to me that here was a clear way of going to work, so that you could cut through this Freudian swamp and say something clearly, instead of wrapping the whole thing up in a rhetoric which is foreign to oneself or which, I think, was in a way foreign to my generation, though my generation hadn't found the proper voice.[23]

The extremes are either "overblown rhetoric" (Dylan Thomas and the Apocalypse) or, what was to emerge in the next decade, "a horribly common style, ... [with] that 'man-of-world' off-handedness, that rather rootless wit" (Larkin and *New Lines*).[24]

Neither extravagance nor vulgarity, on the other hand, has ever constituted part of Tomlinson's moral perspective. He has sought to write of the self without committing the subjectivist sin, and, for all his aesthetic perceptions and foreign cities, is vitally preoccupied with the quality of life in Britain. His settings may on occasion be exotically foreign (Fiascherino, the Château de Muzot, Aix-en-Provence, and Carrara, apart from Arizona, New Mexico, New York, and San Francisco), but it is the Gloucestershire countryside, his home for the past three decades, to which Tomlinson more frequently returns, as in this late poem to the Gloucester-born composer and poet, "To Ivor Gurney":

Driving north, I catch the hillshapes, Gurney,
   Whose drops and rises – Cotswold and Malvern
In their cantilena above the plains –
   Sustained your melody: (*NNY* 27)

Here the musical imagery of cantilena and melody suits the lyricism of Gurney, whether as poet or composer. Nevertheless, following Stevens's commitment to the Northern States (to Pennsylvania and Connecticut), Tomlinson shows how industrial cranes, night-shifts, and Stoke-on-Trent can also prove fruitful to the creative self. Indeed, in "At Stoke" (*CP* 243), the industrial Midlands prove to be the "single landscape" from which all his others have come:

I have lived in a single landscape. Every tone
 And turn have had for their ground
These beginnings in grey-black: a land
 Too handled to be primary – all the same,
The first in feeling.

The function of such "ground," indeed, derives from its several senses: as landscape, certainly, but also as foundation for subsequent work; as reason accounting for that work; and, most appropriately in this instance, in its musical sense as melody or plainsong, and, as used in painting, as main surface or principal colour. Such several senses are all present in the term "ground" – Tomlinson's words frequently have to be unravelled in this way, such multiplicity of meaning capturing in turn the world's variety and constituting one more expression of the poet's preoccupation with roots, whether familial, social, or etymological. Indeed, he has insisted, "The poet must rescue etymology from among the footnotes, thus moving up into the body of the text" (189).

Yet far from romanticizing that industrial landscape, the poet regards it with the same draughtsman's eye he applies to Delft or Venice:

A whitish smoke
in drifting diagonals
accents, divides
the predominance of street
and chimney lines,
where all is either
mathematically supine
or vertical, except
the pyramids of slag.   ("Canal," 64–5)

Moreover, in his 1975 Royal Society of Literature lecture, "The Poet as Painter," Tomlinson attested to the persistent influence of that childhood landscape:

the Midlands were always present as one term in a dialectic, as a demand for completeness subconsciously impelling the forms of one's art, even demanding *two* arts [his poetry and painting] where the paradisal aspect of the visual could perhaps be rescued and celebrated.

Coming back to the Potteries almost thirty years later, I saw how much the world of my poems depended on the place, despite and because of the fact that they were an attempt to find a world of clarities, a world of unhazed senses, an intuition of Edenic freshnesses and clear perceptions. (*Eden* 12)

Tomlinson uses the industrial North to suggest a chillness of air, a wintry perspective, which serves as a useful and necessary balance to the more exotic Mediterranean South. The cold air in the Canadian landscape in "Night Ferry" (*Return* 50) provides a similarly chilling northern counterpoint to the rippling movement of the water, while Tomlinson himself has commented thus: "I had always thought of myself as being temperamentally drawn towards the south. ... Perhaps I am travelling north now to strike a truer balance with my southern proclivity."[25] While it is an antithesis repeated in Wallace Stevens (Florida and Connecticut), it is by no means peculiarly American: the tension is acute in the work of Thomas Mann, for example, between the Northern European and the Mediterranean vision, and it proved a similar aesthetic dilemma earlier for both Keats and Tennyson. The question is the subject for three fine early Tomlinson poems, "Tramontana at Lerici," "Northern Spring," and "At Holwell Farm." The direction in all three poems is towards disparities and detachment: recognizing and valuing the distinctness of things, and achieving a similar impersonality oneself. Appropriately enough, in "Tramontana at Lerici" the perspective moves from the second-person pronoun "you" to the impersonal third-person "one," as the cold tramontane wind chills an "air / Unfit for politicians and romantics":

Leaf-dapples sharpen. Emboldened by this clarity
    The minds of artificers would turn prismatic,
Running on lace perforated in crisp wafers
    That could cut like steel. Constitutions,
Drafted under this fecund chill, would be annulled
    For the strictness of their equity, the moderation of their pity. (*CP* 27)

Such clarity is matched in the geometrical imagery of "Canal" or in the balance of opposites achieved in the Dutch interior in "At Delft." The landscape is a moral one, descriptive of a state of mind as much as an external view, and the chillness of air, like the necessary distancing, impersonality, or detachment, incorporates, distinguishes, and defines, rather than denies and excludes. The artificers' minds "turn prismatic" rather than remain merely one-dimensional. (Tomlinson employs a similar image in a late poem, "The Double Rainbow" [316].)

Likewise, in "Northern Spring" (28) the "confusion" of the natural world, like the "instructive frenzy" of Van Gogh ("Farewell to Van Gogh," 36), is less extravagant than "medicinal":

> Nor is this the setting for extravagance. Trees
>   Fight with the wind, the wind eludes them
> Streaking its cross-lanes over the uneasy water
>   Whose bronze whitens, To emulate such confusion
> One must impoverish the resources of folly,
>   But to taste it is medicinal.

Nevertheless, amongst "the profusion of possibilities" an imagined house counterbalances "The variegated excess" and makes definition possible. Van Gogh, though thanked, is bid farewell; the Northern spring, for all its confusion, proves a valuable moral agent, encouraging discipline and endurance: "Evening, debauching this sky, asks / To be appraised and to be withstood."

"At Holwell Farm," the third and finest of these poems, is beautifully shaped, organized so as to capture in its structure and technique precisely that conjunction of "temperate sharpness" which distinguishes the autumnal season. The terms are those of Keats in his famous letter to John Hamilton Reynolds (21 September 1819), written two days after composing the ode "To Autumn." "How beautiful the season is now – How fine the air. A temperate sharpness about it. Really, without joking, chaste weather – Dian skies – I never lik'd stubble fields so much as now – Aye better than the chilly green of the spring. Somehow a stubble plain looks warm."[26] In its persistent search for the essential nature of things, in its stress upon definition and shaping disparities, Tomlinson's vision may thus be paralleled in Keats as well as in other poets and painters. Such Keatsian marriage of contraries is also, however, distinctively a feature of Tomlinson's own search for meaning and the appropriate "language of sense" and, for all its debt to the Romantic, the poem proves successful and moving in its own right.

The poet captures the particularly ambivalent character of the season, with autumn reflecting the warmth and fulfilment of summer and presaging the cold and deathlike stasis of winter. As such, the season stands at a threshold, frontier, or vortex-point, capable of marrying the contrary states in a synthesis which sharpens one's awareness of all seasons, of the natural cyclism, and of time itself. The poet may begin then by observing an autumn fire but moves outwards from the fire's core to the stone farmhouse, to consideration of the house's several functions, and to an examination of Wordsworthian "natural piety." The fire's core radiates brightness but it is the autumnal chill, "a quality of air, a temperate sharpness," which makes all possible. The "kindred flame" in the stone (whether the stone of the fireplace reddening in the heat or the sun giving a distinctive warmth to the exterior stone walls) images the poet's awareness of resemblances or correspondences. But extending beyond purely aesthetic observation, the experience possesses social and moral relevance: we are dealing with the utilities of actual life; the farm serves also as house and dwelling, and becomes a symbol of order, stability and permanence.[27] The season and its air may indicate the temporal flux, brought to a moment of fulfilment or perfection, but by definition the flux brings change and decay; our appreciation of autumn depends upon our awareness of the other seasons also, upon our definition of time, upon our sharpness of perspective. The house serves to balance time's ravages, and the conjunctions of warmth and chill, flame, fruit, and stone, are set against the rootedness of the house. Natural piety is put aside as irrelevant to both builder and poet; what both those figures share, on the other hand, is the awareness of "sharp disparities" and the need to organize, shape, and, discerning "the Eden image," celebrate the "quality of air."

> Crude stone
> By a canopy of shell, each complements
>   In opposition, each is bound
> Into a pattern of utilities – this farm
>   Also a house, this house a dwelling.
> Rooted in more than earth, to dwell
>   Is to discern the Eden image, to grasp
> In a given place and guard it well
>   Shielded in stone. Whether piety
> Be natural, is neither the poet's
>   Nor the builder's story, but a quality of air,
> Such as surrounds and shapes an autumn fire
>   Bringing these sharp disparities to bear. (39)

# CHAPTER TWO

# Definition and Understanding

In Octavio Paz's words, Tomlinson "does not seek the 'thing in itself' or the 'thing in myself' but rather things in that moment of indecision when they are on the point of generation or degeneration. The moment they appear or disappear before us, before they form as objects in our minds or dissolve in our forgetfulness" (*BW* 8). In his search, Tomlinson adopts a language of sense in which the drawing of distinctions, seeing both affinities and disparities, leads through appraisal and recognition to understanding. The question of definition is frequently posed: "To define the sea – / We change our opinions / With the changing light" (*CP* 6). Since the changing light affects the world's colours, some shading off, others remaining stubbornly themselves, our opinions change likewise. Moreover, definition can also discomfort – "At evening, one is alarmed by such definition" (27) – and depends upon another vital act of mind, the drawing of distinctions. Definition too is subject to change: in a recent volume, the poet describes the sea's tide-edge seeming to form a face's profile in its contact with the rock cliff:

> The face comes imaging up from chaos
>   Just where the bedrock forces water
> To an instant of definition, lost
>   Till the next wave meets with white
> The same resistance. (*NNY* 45)

Better, definition is subject to redefinition, to constant inconstancy, changing with the changing light, with new perspectives and vistas, with increased awareness and perpetual reassessment. It may be that the terms "definition" and "distinctions" appear more frequently in Tomlinson's earliest volumes (up to *A Peopled Landscape* in 1963), but the process of defining, clarifying, seeing the whole and real, remains central to his persistent preoccupation not just with perception but with vision, with how one is led through perception to penetrate the essences of things. To know the world as event is to participate in dynamic interchange with the world; in order for that interchange to reveal the real, it requires constant appraisal and the exercise of judgment.

Tomlinson's world is thus multifarious, dazzlingly full of reflections and refractions, fluctuations and distinctions; indeed, he frequently defines by way of negatives, by saying what a thing is not:

The afternoon violet
Is not so unthinkably itself,
Nor does that imperceptibly greening light
Freeze so remotely in its own essence
As this yellow.

> ("Eight Observations on the Nature of Eternity," *CP* 5)

Defining what a thing is not is one way of establishing its essence, and in his "version" of Machado's "The Ilexes" the technique is used brilliantly:

And you
        of the rustic stance? –
                the ashen trunk that has
neither grace nor arrogance
        and branches
                that are colourless;
"verdurous" would not
        describe your leaves
                (swart ilexes)
nor catch your vigour
        without strain and your
                humility that's firmness.
Nothing
        shines
                in the round

spread summit –
    neither
        your foliage
that's green-obscure
    nor the yellow green
        that marks your flower.
There's
    nothing
        handsome or superb
or warlike
    in your bearing,
        and in your mood
no petulance:   (*CI* 13–14)

"Neither," "nor," "nothing," "no" – each defines finely the ilexes' essential nature; each acquires, through careful modulation of rhythm and precise positioning in the lines, a centrality which manages to convert the negatives into an affirming positive.[1] One might even suggest that the negative definition matches Machado's Hardy-like austerity, detachment, and admiration of solitude and the suffering solitary, with which qualities Wordsworth's resolution and independence also belong.

Definition, however, is further achieved through the precise attention Tomlinson pays to perspective, to the prismatic or geometrical character of a perception. To pursue another analogy, experience takes on a near-molecular structure, dynamic in its chemistry, multifaceted, organic. His correspondences and distinctions are never static or two-dimensional, but copious, alert to the interplay of shifting light and shade. "Paring the Apple" thus uses a characteristically everyday occurrence as illustration, and, by the poem's conclusion, we appreciate the need for "recognition," for the blade's incisive edge, for the movement to the interior, whether in portraits and still-lifes or in the paring of an apple. Indeed, the poem's structure, line divisions, rhythms, as well as particular word choice, all combine with the physical act of paring to reinforce the process of revelation being defined, upheld, and practised:

There are portraits and still-lifes.

And there is paring the apple.

And then? Paring it slowly,
From under cool-yellow
Cold-white emerging. And ...?

The spring of concentric peel
Unwinding off white,
The blade hidden, dividing.

There are portraits and still-lifes
And the first, because "human"
Does not excel the second, and
Neither is less weighted
With a human gesture, than paring the apple
With a human stillness.

The cool blade
Severs between coolness, apple-rind
Compelling a recognition. (*CP* 30)

A similarly precise description of the process of recognition is offered in a late "Prose Poem" (288). The poet seeks to unstopper a nineteenth-century apothecary's jar. The manoeuvre is intricate but ultimately successful, and those involved in it test the jar against their ears for a "dialogue between air and ear."

What had to be done
If we were to undo it, was to pass
   A silk cord round the collar of glass
And rub it warm – but this friction
   Must be swift enough not to conduct its heat
Inside – the best protection against which
   (Only a third hand can ensure this feat)
Is a cube of ice on top of the stopper.
   Whether it was the rubbing only, or the warm
Grasp that must secure the bottle's body,
   The stopper, once more refusing at first,
Suddenly parted – breathed-out
   (So to speak) by the warmed expanding glass.

Like Stevens's more famous, although considerably less concrete, jar in Tennessee ("Anecdote of the Jar"), Tomlinson's provokes relationship – between jar and stopper, between past, present, and future, between jar and owner, also between the two pairs of hands needed to manoeuvre the jar open, between jar and ear, but also between contemplation and use, poetry and prose. Not the least of these relationships is between poet and friends, in a poem written explicitly for the latter. Likewise, Tomlinson has declared, "I always want to unfold the subject, lift it up into consciousness as far as I can, see its facets, set it into a perspective of place and time."[2] It is a perspective which dominates his bilingual sonnet sequence, *Airborn*, written jointly with Paz and organized on the themes of House and Day. Again, the relevance of the title of a later volume, *The Way In*, should be self-evident: he has persistently sought a "way in" to essence, into the individuality of self and into the otherness of things. He made a similar point about place in "The Insistence of Things," a prose poem derived from journal entries:

It takes so long to become aware of the places we inhabit. Not so much of the historic or geographic facts attaching to them, as of the moment to moment quality of a given room, or of the simple recognitions that could be lured to inhabit a paragraph, a phrase, a snatch of words – and thus speak to us. (261)

Place and its "moment to moment quality" come together in a superb, slightly later poem, "Departure" (289).

The poet focuses upon a particular moment and place, a point of departure when friends, before leaving on their journey, turn once again to see the brook which flows through the poet's garden. The place's significance is evident: Tomlinson has written frequently and affectionately of his Gloucestershire cottage and its surrounding Severnside landscape. However, time joins with place to confer meaning upon the seemingly trivial action: for the friends have little time left; the stream is appropriately in spate; and at the time of writing, their jet plane traces a similarly rapid and evanescent trail. Yet the friends "turned on" themselves – that is, changed direction, reversed themselves, but, in a poem which is preoccupied with recognition and definition in the midst of change, the poet's phrase includes also a turning-in upon one's self which brings renewal, an action the poet himself repeats in his conclusion.

You were to leave and being all but gone,
    Turned on yourselves, to see that stream
Which bestows a flowing benediction and a name
    On our house of stone. Late, you had time
For a glance, no more, to renew your sense
    Of how the brook – in spate now –
Entered the garden, pooling, then pushing
    Over a fall, to sidle a rock or two
Before it was through the confine.

The friends' departure enhances their knowledge of themselves, this place and time, and their relationship with the poet. Indeed, for all its emphasis upon time and flux, the poem is in fact rooted in relationship, acknowledges the problem of expression and communication, and overcomes that problem with description. The description is again marvellously precise, at the same time conversational and intimate in tone, yet so gaining in significance that the climax fleshes out, by way of concrete images, subtle rhythms and syntax, the very perception itself. The focus upon the mental processes in action justifies Tomlinson's own parallel between his work and that of Wordsworth and Coleridge, and leads to what in the Romantic tradition would be freely admitted as a numinous experience:

        it is here
    That I like best, where the waters disappear
Under the bridge-arch, shelving through coolness,
    Thought, halted at an image of perfection
Between gloom and gold, in momentary
    Stay, place of perpetual threshold,
Before all flashes out again and on
    Tasseling and torn, reflecting nothing but sun.

Thought, like time and the brook, are held here "in momentary / Stay" – the enjambement once more serves effectively to capture the sense of a still point of a turning world (to use Eliot's terms), held appropriately enough in "perpetual threshold" at a point "Between gloom and gold." For the imagery of "threshold," like that of frontier, reflects exactly the fluctuating nature of Tomlinson's world, things appearing and disappearing, but also his entry within, crossing thresholds into essences and so gaining understanding.

Tomlinson himself has acknowledged[3] two dominant themes in his eighth volume, *The Way In* – that of place and that of the return, and indeed both themes are central to his most recent volume, *The Return*. Certainly his sense of place is as heightened as that of William Carlos Williams or D.H. Lawrence or, for that matter, William Wordsworth, and recurs throughout his work, as notable in *Notes from New York* (1984) and *The Return* (1987) as in *The Necklace* (1955). As one critic has perceptively noted, "Among [Tomlinson's] most potent words are 'where,' 'here,' 'there.' "[4] Likewise, in an earlier comment upon *A Peopled Landscape*, Tomlinson wrote: "most of my poems seem to grow out of very definite places and even in the 'Ode to Arnold Schoenberg,' which celebrates a discovery international in application, namely the twelve-tone system, Gloucestershire church bells and cockcrows insist upon being heard in the piece."[5] Recognitions are again compelled. It is also a recognition he praises in the work of the contemporary French poet Philippe Jaccottet, in whose poetry "humanity and landscape are held in imaginative rapport." "At a time when our own poetry has too often the appearance of being in the hands of moral grotesques, Jaccottet's exploration of what we mean by a landscape, a place, a centre, takes on present and future relevance for us."[6]

In his own search for such relevance, Tomlinson employs recurrent imagery of cave, centre, or interior (such as the apple paring or jar opening reveal), but refuses to mythologize: as he advised in "The Farmer's Wife" (71),

> Distrust
> that poet who must symbolize
> your stair into
> an analogue
> of what was never there.
> Fact
> has its proper plenitude
> that only time and tact
> will show, renew.

Yeatsian mythologizing, as much as Stevens's opulence and elegance, leads to inaccuracy. Instead, the poet trusts to "time and tact," the latter embracing not only consideration and discretion, both of the object and the person, but also discrimination, taste, sensibility, balance, and not the least the good sense which comes from touch or, in less literal terms, grasping the meaning of a thing. "Fact," as opposed to hyperbole and mythologizing, is not lacking in "its proper plenitude." Similarly, then, in "The Cavern" (120–1), the central image may be a North American underground canyon, as much a place for descent into some primeval darkness of self as are E.M. Forster's Marabar caves, but the poem begins on a characteristically negative, even debunking note:

Obliterate
mythology as you unwind
this mountain-interior
into the negative-dark mind,
as there
the gypsum's snow
the limestone stair
and boneyard landscape grow
into the identity of flesh.

The imagery is that of photography, appropriate to the tourist making his descent, camera at the ready, although its source more likely lies in Tomlinson's early interest in film. The anthropomorphic qualities of the rock (nostrils, eyes, faces, feet) establish "chill affinities," while at the same time retaining the rock's essential inhumanity. The descent into the interior, with its architecture of curtain, arch, and buttress, is nevertheless analogous to the necessary descent of the self and the mysterious matrix which is the self's "home":

Not far
enough from the familiar,
press
in under a deeper dark until
the curtained sex
the arch, the streaming buttress
have become
the self's unnameable and shaping home.

The title poem of *The Shaft* (306–7) offers a similar descent, this time down a disused mine, into subterranean darkness, complemented by the cover photograph of a shaft of sunlight. The ambiguity is obvious; moreover, as the poet himself has pointed out further meanings, the mine shaft is both natural and historical, "at once a place that nature had reclaimed beneath growth and water, and an image of human endeavour threatened, of time menacing men."[7]

> The shaft seemed like a place of sacrifice:
>     You climbed where spoil heaps from the hill
> Spilled out into a wood, the slate
>     Tinkling underfoot like shards, and then
> You bent to enter: a passageway:
>     Cervix of stone: the tick of waterdrops,
> A clear clepsydra: and squeezing through
>     Emerged into cathedral space, held-up
> By a single rocksheaf, a gerbe
>     Buttressing-back the roof.

The shaft is thus "like a place of sacrifice"; also a place of birth, initiation and rebirth ("Cervix of stone"), it opens into a "cathedral space." It is associated with time and with organic growth through its analogues – of a water-clock or "clepsydra," "rocksheaf," and "gerbe." But it also threatens, its workings now submerged in water but still offering "A vertigo that dropped through centuries / To the first who broke into these fells: / The shaft was not a place to stare into / Or not for long." These descents, then, reveal a landscape similar to those of Tomlinson's later collages, which describe, as Octavio Paz has argued, "an imaginary landscape" and offer instead of a mythology "a fantastic morphology" (*BW* 13). And indeed Tomlinson has concerned himself throughout with both form and metamorphosis (the morphology of biology) but also with the forms of words and their inflexions (the morphology of philology). Morphology, moreover, involves evolution and change, both of which relate to Tomlinson's concern for the self's maturation. Similarly, when he wrote of his early contact with the work of the American painter Georgia O'Keeffe, he was struck by the form of her landscapes: "In it [*The Mountain*], all the sinews of the mountain stood revealed. It seemed to have heaved upward and fallen sideways like a sleeper who has just turned over. And yet it was not in any way personified." Instead, he noted "the firm articulation of the musculature, the rock-thrust, the held declivities, the sense of an even light bringing the whole to bear" (*Some Americans* 76–7). Affinities are sought, then, but not personification or mythologizing; the recognition or understanding comes from descent into the centre or essential being, a perception of the whole from the inside.

While Tomlinson's collages belong to a later period, the descent towards essence is present in his poetry from the outset, with the interior portrayed as both cold and hard – "the cold centre" (*CP* 10), "a fragility whose centre / Is hard" (38). Such hardness is present in recurrent imagery of stone – obdurate, resistant, permanent – particularly when it has been worked by man into houses or walls or sculpture. His own graphics include stone shapes; his world, while often considerably sensuous, even opulent, is possessed of that same sharp spiky outline upheld by Blake. Indeed, for all his many landscapes and highly developed descriptive powers, Tomlinson no more worships Nature than did Blake: "Nature is blind / Like habit," he declared early ("Reflections," 18), and can be "improved" ("Suggestions for the Improvement of a Sunset," 6), as Stevens also argued.[8] And while clarity of perception, as we have seen, is matched by a parallel chillness of air, a lucidity which has a keenness and edge to it, all such terms describe that precision the poet himself continually seeks. The search for "the cold centre" can be undertaken successfully only by those imaginative selves who in turn possess the requisite acuteness of sight and candour of spirit.

A more satisfying image in *The Way of the World*, replacing the earlier abstract "centre," is the skull. In a superb poem, "To be Engraved on the Skull of a Cormorant" (187–8), the poet recaptures the fragility and delicateness both of the bird's skull and of the artist's engraving technique. Like Blake, he employs the engraving process to image the insight (here "reticence") both artist and perceiver must achieve. Such reticence demands a paring-down, like that of the apple earlier, bringing an awareness of the essential thing caught there in its skullshape. For "reticence" means, literally, "to be silent," a quality shared by the cormorant skull and sought, after Mallarmé, by the aspiring poet. The quality is caught in the poem's shape and form, but particularly in a manner repeated elsewhere in Tomlinson, by the simple use of hyphen and enjambement ("still- / perfect"), and by the Stevensian prosaic, disyllabic, two-stressed line, "but be." In the poet's eyes, such reticence brings definition and understanding and involves a union of self and object. That union is reflected in the poet-painter's marriage of theme and form, in the poem's narrow shape and precise short stresses.

across the thin
façade, the galleried-
with-membrane-head:
narrowing, to take
the eye-dividing
declivity where
the beginning beak
prepares for flight
in a still-
perfect salience:
here, your glass
needs must stay
steady and your gross
needle re-tip
itself with reticence
but be
as searching as the sea
that picked and pared
this head yet spared
its frail acuity.

Among the graphics in his *Words and Images* (1972) are two skull-shapes – "Horizontal Skull" and "Long Beaked Skull" – and later work like "Three Prehistoric Masks" are in fact also skullshapes.[9] Moreover, in *The Way of the World*, in a prose poem "Skullshapes," the poet applies similar etching technique to "the rural detritus of cattle skulls brought home by children." Like Henry Moore with his elephant skulls or, perhaps more appropriately, Georgia O'Keeffe, with whose paintings of cattle bones Tomlinson has long been familiar (*Some Americans* 86),[10] the poet is fascinated by the skulls' physical properties. More distinctively, he sees their fusion of weight and fragility transformed into "wit" (both the Mozartian lightness of the flute and the possession of intelligence and wisdom):

Washing them of their mottlings, the hand grows conscious of weight, weight sharp with jaggednesses. Suspend them from a nail and one feels the bone-clumsiness go out of them: there is weight still in their vertical pull downwards from the nail, but there is also a hanging fragility. The two qualities fuse and the brush translates this fusion as wit, where leg-like appendages conclude the skulls' dangling mass. (*CP* 191)

Tomlinson's fascination with the geometry of an object or with the architectural character of a perspective has already been noted. His poetic vocabulary is full of angles, planes, verticals; he continually points to a "tree's geometry" (97) or "the valley vineyards' spread geometry" (258) or muses upon "a geometry of water" (155). While the imagery is present in *The Return* (23, 47, 50), geometry tends in the later volumes to give way to imagery of maps. Hence, in "At the Trade Center" (*NNY* 13), the poet is made aware from the Manhattan sky-scraper's height of

> The map of land, the map of air:
>    Rivers both sides of this island
> Tug the gaze askance from the grid of streets
>    To the sea- and bird-ways, the expanse
> That drinks the reverberation of these energies.

Whether involving geometry or map, Tomlinson's gaze is constantly being tugged askance, drawn along lines of vista, mapping with grids and shaping order through boundaries, whether the discipline of the stanza or of the rhyme or the building of a wall. Moreover, following Blake, he is drawn to "declivities" and contours because these delineate, draw distinctions and limits, enclose like walls, create shape and order. Hence the poet's eye follows the definition brought about by that most indefinite of things, the actions of mist upon a landscape. "Mistlines flow slowly in, filling the land's declivity that lay unseen until that indistinctness had acknowledged them" (*CP* 189; cf. 233, verse version). On another occasion, provoked by the evening scent of hay, the "Dark incense of a solar sacrament," he notes "Where, laid in swathes, the field-silk dulls and dries / To contour out the land's decliv-ities" (323). His eye is persistently attentive to lines and circles, ditches and field-lines, hill-shapes. Such lines are also "lines of force," describe a "weave" – another variation on the imagery of skeins and meshing – and lead to centres which maintain their otherness:

> Edges are centres: once you have found
>    Their lines of force, the least of gossamers
> Leads and frees you, nets you a universe
>    Whose iridescent weave shines true
> Because you see it, but whose centre is not you:   ("At the Edge," 324)

A similar tracing of lines of perspective is present in Tomlinson's graphics, particularly evident in *Words and Images* and the early examples in *In Black and White* (plates 1–6). Moreover, the lines contribute to the movement of the painting, creating a multidimensional quality, but also engaging the observer's eye, like a thread, drawing him into the object. The technique parallels that of the nineteenth-century American painter Thomas Eakins, in Tomlinson's own description of the model's pose:

> To her dress
> by the intersections
> of the grid he tied
> coloured ribbons, thus
> projecting her
> like an architect's elevation
> on a plane
> that was vertical, the canvas
> at a right angle
> to the eye and perpendicular
> to the floor.   ("A Garland for Thomas Eakins," III, *CP* 140)

The connection with his thread imagery is clear and maintained. In *The Shaft*, for example, Tomlinson shows how the hill-line contours of a landscape and the acute observer's eye, hand and words combine to create an experience of perfection:

> Word and world rhyme
>     As the penstrokes might if you drew
> The spaciousness reaching down through a valley view,
>     Gathering the lines into its distances
> As if they were streams, as if they were eye-beams:
>     Perfect, then, the eye's command in its riding,
> Perfect the coping hand, the hillslopes
>     Drawing it into such sight the sight would miss,
> Guiding the glance the way perfection is.   ("Rhymes," 290)

Both imagery of thread and eye and the theme of creative transformation come together in a subsequent poem in the same volume, "The Metamorphosis," describing a fellside of bluebells. The flowers follow the contours of a now dried-up stream, flowing with "imaginary water," an illusion created by both bluebells finding out "each tributary thread" of the stream bed and by Tomlinson's characteristically dishevelling wind:

> So that the mind, in salutary confusion,
>   Surrendering up its powers to the illusion,
>     Could, swimming in metamorphoses, believe
>   Water itself might move like a flowing of flowers. (292)

The imagery is wholly characteristic, as we shall see in a subsequent chapter: Tomlinson frequently characterizes the creative self as swimming, with water the element not only of flux but of origins and metamorphosis. Hence, the "confusion" to which the mind is brought is "salutary," allowing for reshaping of self and experience in new and increasingly real perception.

An experience, like a landscape vista, the architecture of a house, or a skullshape, is thus carefully dissected, analysed, and reconstructed. The clarity, necessary to such an examination, parallels the detachment or impersonality the poet also promotes. Each of these in turn, however, is achieved not by retreating into stasis or transcendence, any more than the poet wishes the Romantic agony. Whatever his Augustanism, Tomlinson's promotion of clarity, order, and permanence is founded upon a characteristically Romantic awareness of the temporal flux. That flux is never evaded, always endured, and, on certain occasions at least, celebrated in near-religious fashion. Indeed, Tomlinson's world must of necessity be one of flux: the shifting light and colours, the changes in weather and season, the imaginative perception itself, the recognition of resemblances and "répétition," the "negotiation" occurring between perceiver and perceived – all these demand a dynamism, a world of event or of instress or energy which Tomlinson admired in his early masters, Hopkins and Blake. Determined then to avoid the stasis of a still-life or of transcendence, he frequently attends to the world's dialectic. Describing his very early "poem in folio," *Solo for a Glass Harmonica*, with its "starting-point" in two works by Mozart, he noted that "the moral interest of the piece" derives from the dialectical opposition of elements (here "the confrontation of dullness and volatile wit"). Likewise, of the world a volume of poetry creates, he proceeded to explain:

I have attempted to make [that world] as sharp in its forms as a Hokusai print and as definite in its colouring. Indeed, the extra-literary influences of which I am most conscious are visual art and the cinema. Poetry moves through time like the cinema. That is why it is necessary for the poet who has felt the influence of the painter to avoid the genre of the literary still life, to prevent a stasis among the elements of his poem. The hardness of crystals, the facets of cut glass; but also the shifting of light, the energizing weather which is the result of the combination of sun and frost – these are the images for a certain mental climate, components for the moral landscape of my poetry in general.[11]

The argument reveals the poet's characteristic emphasis upon that definition which becomes possible only through the tension of dialectical opposites – the "sharp disparities" of which he showed himself aware in "At Holwell Farm" (39). Likewise, in "Winter Encounters" (17–18), "The ceaseless pairings" ("House and hollow; village and valley-side," roof and cloud, the "brisk exchanges" whether between the people sheltering by the wall or between inanimate objects) all "articulate the sense" and make one aware of the dialectic running through all things: "Calmness within the wind, the warmth in cold." Again, in the conjunction of fire and water, in "Steel: the night shift" (68), he sees "a principle, a pulse / in all these molten and metallic contraries, / this sweat unseen." For all its geometrical or crystallized quality, then, Tomlinson's vision remains dynamic and dialectical, preferring that "energizing weather" of which he spoke in *Solo for a Glass Harmonica*, a weather "which is a result of the combination of sun and frost."

Frequently the dialectic is expressed in a tension between the impermanence and cyclism of the seasons and man's desire for roots, for a stability capable of withstanding the destructive element in which he lives. Consequently, the battle is often represented between a house and wind, weather or season – "the choreography of the season," as the poet calls it ("Autumn Piece," 218) and which in another, "The Flood" (346–8), involves the severe testing of his Gloucestershire cottage, "Our ark of stone." The same sense of movement, of a dance of the elements, is present in his graphics. Avoiding, however, the Romantic apocalyptic tone present in Ted Hughes (for example, his early poem, "Wind," in *The Hawk in the Rain* [1957], Tomlinson focuses upon the mental process rather than, as Hughes does, upon capturing the very physicality of the experience. Hence, in the fine title poem, "The Way of a World"

(165–6), he writes of remembering two past images – a gull and an ash-key seed, both flying through an autumn wind:

Having mislaid it, and then
    Found again in a changed mind
The image of a gull the autumn gust
    Had pulled upwards and past
The window I watched from, I recovered too
    The ash-key, borne-by whirling
On the same surge of air, like an animate thing:

The fact of memory indicates both the mental world of Tomlinson's poetry and that poetry's function to preserve or "recover." Memory also, in a Wordsworthian manner, enables him to achieve the proper degree of detachment and impersonality, to recollect the images in tranquillity. As in Stevens, memory proves a significant factor in the search for resemblances. As the "anarchy / Of air" is balanced against and restrained by the trees' branches, so the mind achieves a similar "counterpoise" and can see gull, ash-key, wind, and tree, indeed the existential battle, within the proper perspective. The experience, like life itself, is shaped and given an order and a purpose. Neither transcendence nor absolutisim is sought, because it is change itself which enables us to perceive the order in disorder, the overriding purpose which remains constant within change:

In all these evanescences of daily air,
    It is the shapes of change, and not the bare
Glancing vibrations, that vein and branch
    Through the moving textures: we grasp
The way of a world in the seed, the gull
    Swayed toiling against the two
Gravities that root and uproot the trees.

The poem marries, by way of memory and the power of intellection, the meditative intelligence with the aesthetic eye. The foundation for that marriage, as Octavio Paz has seen, is the world of flux, the temporal essence, and, through his constant search for relationship, Tomlinson's participation in that world or essence. "In Tomlinson's poetry," Paz writes, "the perception of movement is exquisite and precise.

Whether the poem is about rocks, plants, sand, insects, leaves, birds or human beings, the true protagonist, the hero of each poem, is change." And "change," Paz adds significantly, "means relationship" (*BW* 10). For what the imaginative self in "The Way of a World" perceives is not chaos ("Glancing vibrations") but "the shapes of change." "We grasp / The way of a world," the poet states, using his characteristic verb of contact or relationship, since "grasp" includes both physical touch and intellectual recognition and understanding. The self grasps the existential flux through its own shaping and ordering, through its awareness of relationships, through recollection and through its own achieved unity or identity.

Tomlinson has from the beginning been aware of the fallacious and dead quality of stasis: "A static instance, therefore untrue" ("Sea Change," 7); "Silencing movement, / They withdraw life" ("Through Binoculars," 7). The mercurial self, like the encompassing eye, feeds on change, not out of Romantic restlessness but because existence is continual process. But as we see from one of his several prose poems included in *The Way of a World* and serving to define and make concrete the poet's preoccupations, process is "A process; procession; trial" (193–4). It involves "A process of weather, a continuous changing"; but also a delineation of limits, a defining of boundaries, "to walk the bounds to lay claim to them, knowing all they exclude"; "A procession, a body of things proceeding," which involves also "metamorphosis"; and, what might be conceived as the climax of such processes, "A trial," an appropriately legal term given the poet's commitment to the "judicious eye" and to balance and impartiality:

A trial: the whole of the proceedings, including the complication and the unravelling. One accords the process its reality, one does not deify it; inserted among it, one distinguishes and even transfigures, so that the quality of vision is never a prisoner of the thing seen. The beginnings have to be invented: thus the pictograph is an outline, which nature, as the poet said, does not have.[12] And the ends? The ends are windows opening above that which lay unperceived until the wall of the house was completed at that point, over that sea.

All four elements – earth, air, fire, and water – are subject to process, though perhaps air and water best reflect change, earth being more the element of rootedness and dogged endurance, while fire is traditionally associated with alchemical metamorphosis. Certainly Tomlinson is preoccupied particularly with air and water as being those elements in which the existential flux is most acutely evident. However, as he has described growing up in the Potteries, "Air was an element that yet had to be created there." "So of the four elements it was water that held the imagination of the child as growing artist – water fire-tinged, water promising a cleansing, an imaginative baptism, rocking, eddying, full of metamorphoses" (*Eden* 11). Initiation, cleansing, and metamorphosis, then, but, as with his definition of process, Tomlinson also sees the constancy which is the underlying pattern within the stream's flow. Consequently, in "Written on water," the last of a six-part poem called "Movements" (*CP* 236–7), the poet follows the labyrinthine meandering of a stream. It is surely the same stream we have followed already in "Departures," that which is named in the poet's Brook Cottage address, and which overflows in December spate in the title poem of his late volume, *The Flood*. Once more, then, the poet's eye returns, compelled, as if drawn threadlike, to the stream's dialectical progress:

> One returns to it, as though it were a thread
> > Through the labyrinth of appearances, following-out
> By eye, the stream in its unravelling,

The labyrinthine path leads, appropriately enough, to another Tomlinson still centre, a pool the depth and silence of which serve to bring not only definition of self but a religious or visionary sense, that recovery of a paradisal vision which he seeks throughout both his poetry and his painting.

> We lived
> In a visible church, where everything
> > Seemed to be at pause, yet nothing was:
> The surface puckered and drew away
> > Over the central depth; the foliage
> Kept up its liquid friction
> > Of small sounds, their multiplicity
> A speech behind speech, continuing revelation
> > Of itself, never to be revealed:

While Tomlinson's image of "a visible church" is derived from Kant, it is wholly characteristic of the poet's commitment to mutability and the physical world that Kant's ideal society or "ethical commonwealth" should reveal itself through the musical relationship of air and water.[13] The final phrases, however, are reminiscent of Wordsworth's lines on crossing the Alps, when he was made sensible of "woods decaying, never to be decayed, / The stationary blasts of waterfalls" (*The Prelude* [1805], VI, 557–8) – and indeed the same vision of the interpenetration of time and eternity is present in Tomlinson's lines. And, as with Wordsworth, the vision derives from an awareness of a certainty, constancy, or permanence within that very medium, water, which seems least likely to reflect those qualities. Yet the poet proceeds with a further Romantic echo or variation, this time of Keats's epitaph ("Here lies one whose name was writ in water"):

> It rendered new (time within time)
>     An unending present, travelling through
> All that we were to see and know:
>     "Written on water," one might say
> Of each day's flux and lapse,
>     But to speak of water is to entertain the image
> Of its seamless momentum once again,
>     To hear in its wash and grip on stone
> A music of constancy behind
>     The wide promiscuity of acquaintanceship,
> Links of water chiming on one another,
>     Water-ways permeating the rock of time.

The "seamless momentum" of the stream reflects its flux and momentary contact with stone or bank – that very momentariness is captured in a marvellously precise phrase, "The wide promiscuity of acquaintanceship." Yet behind is heard "A music of constancy," imaged further by "Links of water chiming" and, ultimately, "permeating the rock of time."

It is this awareness of a "music of constancy" inherent in time and flux which makes Tomlinson distinguish between stillness and stasis, between certainty and absolutism. Absolutism and transcendence are merely forms of extremism, as evasive as suicide or apocalypse. "We have lived through apocalypse too long," the poet declares firmly ("Prometheus," 156–7); he is likewise aware of the temptations of

"Libido," "the dionysian sluice of the applause," or of being "laurelled in vatic lather" ("A Dream," 157–8). Prometheus, Danton, Scriabin, Blok, Trotsky's assassin – all are "men of extremes" (157) against whom he has continued to warn.[14] "For Danton," a later poem (278–9), describes the French revolutionary once more as a Promethean figure encouraged to Romantic excess and superhuman dreams, returning in this case to his birthplace prior to his arrest and death. Tomlinson thus has Danton experience in a momentary suspension of time a "contrary perfection" he has no time to taste; again the medium by which revelation comes is water, here revealing also the revolutionary's inevitable fall:

> Before he catches in the waterchime
> The measure and the chain a death began,
> And fate that loves the symmetry of rhyme
> Will spring the trap whose teeth must have a man.

The coincidence of sound ("waterchime") points to another fatal, fateful coincidence (the "symmetry" which will require Danton's death by Robespierre as Danton previously had sought the death of the French king and, in time, result also in Robespierre's execution). Time and mutability prove ultimately superior, bringing destruction to Promethean dreams. "The time," on the other hand, as Tomlinson warns in "Against Extremity," "is in love with endings," and elevates poets like Anne Sexton and Sylvia Plath as its heroines. Instead of extremism, he recommends moderation and endurance in characteristic imagery of negotiation, treaties, and bridges, imagery which points ultimately to relationship:

> Let there be treaties, bridges,
>     Chords under the hands, to be spanned
> Sustained: extremity hates a given good
>     Or a good gained.   ("Against Extremity," 163)

His recommendation is founded upon an awareness of the possible: time and change bring definition and certainty, and, ultimately, a quality of being which remains "A possession that is not to be possessed":

Against extremity, let there be
  Such treaties as only time itself
Can ratify, a bond and test
  Of sequential days, and like the full
Moon slowly given to the night,
  A possession that is not to be possessed.

Such possession resists containment or domination, remains a property
of knowledge and understanding, and is thus distinguishable from that
illusory vatic "possession" associated with extremism. Time, not apocalypse, is the preferred measure; rather than possession, the self must
negotiate treaties with the world; the imagination shapes and discovers
certainty through definition and order – these are the means by which
the poet strives to gain knowledge and understanding, a process he continues to chart with increasing strength and precision.

# CHAPTER THREE

# Initiation into Meaning

In *The Poem as Initiation*,[1] the address Tomlinson delivered at Colgate University in 1967, several of his central themes and images come together: the element of water, man's relationship with an alien element, the ceremony with which man celebrates that relationship, and the definition of self and world which comes through recognition of constancy within change. The poet declared himself at the outset of his address "in defence of ceremony":

The poem, in itself, is a ceremony of initiation. It leads us into and through and out on the other side of an imagined experience. It is a rite of passage through a terrain which, when we look back over it, has been flashed up into consciousness in a way we should scarcely have foreseen. Living as we do in an age of demolition – literally so, in its demolition of fine architecture and in a variety of violences that would sacrifice the fineness of relationships – living in an age of demolition, we tend to be impatient of ceremony.

Tomlinson is conscious of the parallel with W.B. Yeats,[2] whose "Prayer for My Daughter" he quotes, but finds another parallel in the North American Indian. "The poem weighs and measures occasions by calling attention to the intricate meshings of words" and so "dwelling on the inner rhythm of events that is as fundamental and as primitive ... as ritual." The Pawnee ceremony for the crossing of a stream distinguishes the different stages in the relationship between water and traveller, revealing an analogous "dwelling on the inner rhythm of events." The swimmer's own crossing described in Tomlinson's accompanying poem, "Swimming Chenango Lake," involves a similar awareness:

The poem tries to celebrate the fact that the help we gain from alien phenomena – even from water, in which (after all) we can't live – the help is towards relation, towards grasp,[3] towards awareness of all that which we are not, yet of relationship with it. It is a help that teaches us not to try merely to reduce objects to our own image, but to respect their otherness and yet find our way into contact with that otherness. In doing so, we are at once chastened and initiated into a new world of meaning and possibility.

Wholly characteristically, however, Tomlinson admits also the "limits" of ceremony, using another anthropological instance, this time from the Hopi. Brought up to believe that certain masked figures are tribal spirits, the Indian maturing from childhood into youth is confronted with the figures who unmask themselves to reveal his kinsmen: "the ceremonial act is always indicating something greater than itself, something of the indivisible and thick texture of reality, something undefinable, yet out there and around us." "The end of *Swimming Chenango Lake* tries to do something similar: when the naked reality, the spreading, pulsating water takes over from the swimmer, the mask of the poem (so to speak) is being put by, and the elusive reality of the lake, or of life, is admitted back into its own."

The poem begins at a particularly significant moment, a vortex point both in the swimmer's relationship with the lake and in the external world of nature:

Winter will bar the swimmer soon.
    He reads the water's autumnal hesitations
A wealth of ways: it is jarred,
    It is astir already despite its steadiness,
Where the first leaves at the first
    Tremor of the morning air have dropped
Anticipating him, launching their imprints
    Outwards in eccentric, overlapping circles. (*CP* 155)

Moreover, we remember in an earlier poem, "In Winter Woods: 4. Focus" (120), "the mind" is described as "that swimmer, unabashed / by season" and capable of encountering Eden. Likewise, as we have seen in a late poem, "The Metamorphosis" (292), the mind is imaged as "swimming in metamorphoses" and led to reconstructed perception of itself and the world. Here, as the swimmer is poised to dive into

Chenango Lake, autumn too is held momentarily suspended in its irrevocable movement towards winter. The suspension is in fact unreal; the temporal flux brooks no barriers; and, aware of the "geometry of water," the poet sees

                          each
      Liquid variation answerable to the theme
          It makes away from, plays before:
      It is a consistency, the grain of the pulsating flow.

The suspension itself resembles Blake's Moment, the grain his famous Minute Particular, and both are indeed at a vortex point where time and eternity interact.[4] Where Blake's Moment serves to render eternity dynamic, Tomlinson's remains necessarily earthbound. Constancy (or "consistency") is certainly present, but his "grain" is "of the pulsating flow" of time itself. Consequently, as the swimmer plunges into the lake, he establishes contact with the water, with time, and with himself. He becomes aware of the flux, of the water's alien nature or otherness, and of his own solitariness. Tomlinson's lines successfully fuse abstract argument with vivid concrete imagery to convey his meaning convincingly:

      For to swim is also to take hold
          On water's meaning, to move in its embrace
      And to be, between grasp and grasping, free.
          He reaches in-and-through to that space
      The body is heir to, making a where
          In water, a possession to be relinquished
      Willingly at each stroke. The image he has torn
          Flows-to behind him, healing itself,
      Lifting and lengthening, splayed like the feathers
          Down an immense wing whose darkening spread
      Shadows his solitariness:

The initiation the swimmer thus undergoes is into his own humanity, as a questing self but also as a chastened finite being. The water is both alien and related, merciless and merciful; and, like water and time, the swimmer participates in and shapes an experience of a distinctly dialectical nature:

Human, he fronts it and, human, he draws back
   From the interior cold, the mercilessness
That yet shows a kind of mercy sustaining him.
   The last sun of the year is drying his skin
Above a surface a mere mosaic of tiny shatterings,
   Where a wind is unscaping all images in the flowing obsidian,
The going-elsewhere of ripples incessantly shaping.[5]


At the conclusion of his address Tomlinson argued that "We can never *know* all that reality, but the rite of the poem has, so one hopes, brought us into closer relation with it. We put down the book. We put aside the mask. We go on living. But it is the book and it is the mask that bring to bear the mystery and the qualities of the process of living." The argument parallels that of D.H. Lawrence and other Romantics, that in the last resort the world is unknowable, the moment immeasurable because infinitely expansible.[6] More than wishing to maintain a mystery at the heart of things, however, Tomlinson has also insisted on "The resistant presence of objects"[7] or the world's otherness. That otherness, he has argued, requires an "ethic of perception ... distrustful of the drama of personality of which Romantic art had made so much, an ethic where, by trusting to sensation, we enter being, and experience its primal fulness in terms other than those we dictate" (*Eden* 14). It is an ethic he found at the centre of Cézanne's vision and which was praised in turn by Lawrence, Rilke, Wallace Stevens, and William Carlos Williams (9): " 'Cézanne's apples,' says D.H. Lawrence, 'are a real attempt to let the apple exist in its own separate entity, without transfusing it with personal emotion' "; Rilke praised Cézanne's "great and incorruptible ... objectivity of ... gaze" (14). Hence, in his own "Cézanne at Aix," Tomlinson writes of the painter's celebrated mountain simply that "It is" (*CP* 37).

Tomlinson found such awareness of the world's otherness shared by Ezra Pound, and distorted in turn by Eliot and Yeats through "their symbologizing of the objective,"[8] but, worse, wholly ignored by Philip Larkin and the Movement. Consequently, in his controversial review of *New Lines*, Tomlinson objected to "this stale feeling of ordinariness, of second-hand responses throughout."[9] The poets anthologized "show a singular want of vital awareness of the continuum outside themselves, of the mystery bodied over against them in the created universe, which they fail to experience with any degree of sharpness or to embody with any instress or sensuous depth." And using terminology inherited from Blake,[10] he argued: "They seldom for a moment escape beyond the suburban mental ratio which they impose on experience. A poet's sense of objectivity, however, of that which is beyond himself and beyond his mental conceit of himself, and his capacity to realize that objectivity within the artefact is the gauge of his artistry and the first prerequisite of all aesthetic genius."

It was a quality, nevertheless, which Tomlinson found in the early twentieth-century Spanish poet, Antonio Machado: "The poet does not pursue / the fundamental I / but the essential you" (*CI* 42). And such objectivity leads not only to an awareness of otherness but to a heightened definition of self. Hence, regarding *Renga* (1971), his remarkable experiment in poetic collaboration with three other poets in three other languages, Tomlinson writes in retrospection of their unison in what "seemed, at first, a questionable venture ... Would the atmosphere be tense with unresolvable divergencies, and calm be shattered by the inevitable collision of four egos?" (*Renga* 35). "One's fears were groundless," he concludes, partly because "the poem was the thing" but also because such collaboration led not only to extinction of self but, paradoxically, to increased relationship of self and heightened awareness of and relationship to others: "Not that one was any the less oneself: one's self was discovered by the juxtapositions and the confrontations that met it. It was part of a relationship. It was almost an *object*" (35). "Speaking with a communal voice one found – once more – one's self" (37).

Such experience of relationship and otherness does not surprise. Tomlinson's own accuracy and attention to perspective, his geometrical imagery, his detachment and impersonality, his rejection of Romantic extremism and suburban staleness, all prove means by which he has sought to achieve in his own work precisely that objectivity and self-definition. As we have seen, his emphasis upon the object's otherness constituted the basis for his early rejection of Stevens's supreme fiction. As his later prose poem "Tout Entouré de Mon Regard" indicates, the rejection applies also to another early exemplar, to Blake's holding infinity in the palm of his hand.[11] The poem begins by asserting the self's central act of measurement:

Surrounded by your glance – shapes at the circumference of its half-circle staring back into foreground shapes – , you measure the climbing abyss up to the birds that intersect in contrary directions the arc of winter air. (190)

But no matter how much of a "pivot" the observer might feel, Tomlinson concludes by overturning Blake's own supreme fiction of the creative self:

To see, is to feel at your back this domain of a circle, whose power consists in evading and refusing to be completed by you.
   It is infinity sustains you on its immeasurable palm.

The Blakean dictum is turned around: it is infinity which holds the perceiving self in its hand. For "The mind too eagerly marries a half truth," as a later poem from *The Way In*, "Tiger Skull" (259), has it. No matter how complete or close our vision, we can never wholly comprehend life's processes. Consequently, in "How Far," from the same volume, we fail to recognize in the leaves' "bursting into green" the darkness "fermenting at its heart":

   the light is a white lie
   told only to hide the dark
   extent from us
   of a seafloor continent. (259)

Nevertheless, the poet's commitment to wholeness and plenitude remains constant throughout his work, from *The Necklace* (1955) to *The Return* (1987). It constitutes his perpetual reaching towards the marriage of eye and self in "Portrait in Stone" (from *A Peopled Landscape*, *CP* 94) or, in "Words for the Madrigalist" (from *The Way of a World*, *CP* 170), his urging to synaesthetic perception: "Look with the ears," "Hear with the eyes." For, as he has more recently pointed out, such synaesthesia evidences "The whole mind": "In all its roused cells / the whole mind unlocks / whenever eye listens, / whenever ear looks" (*The Return* 45). Octavio Paz has thus accurately described Tomlinson as "a poet whose main faculty of sense in his eyes, but eyes that think" (*BW* 10). One of his finest earlier poems, "Ode to Arnold Schoenberg" (*CP* 103–4), captures this vision precisely and convincingly and constitutes another superb initiation into meaning.

The poem begins with the action of the wind upon a willow and its reflection in the river. The disruption and eventual restoration of both tree and reflection parallel in the physical world the contrapuntal structure of Schoenberg's concerto for violin. The same counterpoint exists in the parallel itself and in the very three-ply line the poem employs. The poem's structure therefore follows, much as the reflection and the music, the same essential path, revealing the same essential meaning.

At its margin
    the river's double willow
        that the wind
variously
    disrupts, effaces
        and then restores
in shivering planes:
    it is
        calm morning.
The twelve notes
    (from the single root
        the double tree)
and their reflection:
    let there be
        unity.

For as the music proceeds contrapuntally, shaping beauty and unity out of dissonance, so too the mind acts upon the perception of the double willow. Moreover, employing his familiar thread imagery, Tomlinson connects both music and landscape to man's finitude. The "thread" of the argument, paralleling the violin strings, is thus matched by the meshing of our "common bonds."

Day. The bell-clang
    goes down the air
and, like a glance
    grasping upon its single thread
        a disparate scene,
crosses and re-creates
    the audible morning.
        All meet at cockcrow
when our common sounds
    confirm our common bonds.

What is at stake is more than an aesthetic or epistemological question: the redefinition of beauty out of the consonance and dissonance of both landscape and music has a fundamentally moral significance. Tomlinson's terms are indeed religious ones, and the conclusion near-visionary. The impulse behind his poetry, however, has always been, like that of Blake, to sharpen and expand our awareness of the world. Moreover, the world's infinite variety is achieved because of, rather than despite, the temporal flux. Here the Schoenberg concerto creates "certainty from possibility," shaping the flux in a way that not only reconciles us to it and to our own finitude, but enables us to see that flux as the source of beauty and order. Our lives are thus given direction and purpose; we are reconciled and enriched.

> But to redeem
>     both the idiom and the instrument
>         was reserved
> to this exiled Jew – to bring
>     by fiat
>         certainty from possibility.
> For what is sound
>     made reintelligible
>         but the unfolded word
> branched and budded,
>     the wintered tree
>         creating, cradling space
> and then
>     filling it with verdure?

Cézanne once more provides parallel commentary. In a statement which Tomlinson quotes approvingly, the painter insisted:

All that we see disperses, vanishes; is it not so? Nature is always the same, but nothing remains of it, nothing of what comes to our sight. Our art ought to give the shimmer of duration with the elements, the appearance of all its changes. It ought to make us taste it eternally ... My canvas joins hands. (*Eden* 13)

The relationship with other – "My canvas joins hands" – is crucial to Tomlinson also. Whether in his graphics or his poetry, he has constantly sought, as he declared at the outset, to render reality "in space made articulate" (*CP* 3). While Georgia O'Keeffe likewise was much taken by the idea of art as "filling a space in a beautiful way,"[12] Tomlinson's early expression is more directly indebted to Cézanne and the French Symbolists. As "The Miracle of the Bottle and the Fishes," one of Tomlinson's latest poems, reveals, space remains a recurrent preoccupation. Inspired by Georges Braque's "Bottle and Fishes," the poet does more than illustrate or comment upon the 1912 painting; his poem works in conjunction with the Braque to show their relationship and the related concerns of both poet and painter. Not knowing yet "which is space and which is substance," Tomlinson writes with familiar imagery,

> the eye must stitch
> each half-seen, separate
> identity together
>
> in a mind delighted and disordered by
> a freshness of the world's own weather.   (*Return* 18)

The direction, then, is towards "reciprocation" so that, despite Braque's "layered darknesses" and the "uncertain year," his conclusion, like Tomlinson's, is to explore and "guess how much of space / for all its wilderness / is both honeycomb and home" (19). As in the "Ode to Arnold Schoenberg," the process involves the creation and the cradling of space, but also the "filling it with verdure." That which is known as other becomes also the medium through which to achieve completeness of self, the perfect relationship within the self and of that self's relationship with the world.

# CHAPTER FOUR

# *"I Have Seen Eden"*

Like Stevens and others before him, Tomlinson is fascinated by the theme of transformation and metamorphosis. His fascination follows naturally from his view of the world – as a world which changes constantly, according to both the shifting light and the subjective perceiver. At the same time that world remains ordered and purposeful, its order and purpose revealed in part through its perpetual transformation. Consequently, in his 1982 Clark Lectures, since collected as *Poetry and Metamorphosis* (1983), Tomlinson groups Dryden's translation of Ovid's *Metamorphoses* with Darwin's *Origin of Species*, the latter "a book which dwells insistently and imaginatively on the universal fact of metamorphosis" (*PM* 4). Indeed, in his final lecture Tomlinson focuses upon the art of translation as involving transformation and also recovery. Critical of "merely journeymen efforts," he prefers the "achieved art" whereby the translators "recover, carry over and transform the energies of past civilization" (72–3). Such transformation in turn extends to the translator, who, in T.S. Eliot's words quoted by Tomlinson, "is giving the original through himself, and finding himself through the original" (76).[1] Octavio Paz has put it similarly: "in translating, we change what we translate and above all that we change ourselves. For us translation is transmutation, metaphor: a form of change and severance; a way, therefore, of ensuring the continuity of our past by transforming it in dialogue with other civilizations" (*Renga* 18).

Tomlinson's own career as a translator thus bears upon his own distinctive theme of transformation. In translating Tyutchev or Machado, Vallejo, Paz, and others, Tomlinson has sought both change and recovery, processes which apply both to his own self and to his own time and place, his society and civilization. But translation not only builds bridges or negotiates with another imaginative self or time or language; it acknowledges differences as well as parallels, permits judicious distinctions, and is related in turn to Tomlinson's preoccupation with otherness. His long-standing contact with poets like William Carlos Williams, Marianne Moore, Louis Zukovsky, and George Oppen has enabled him to incorporate their distinctive use of the line unit, particularly the Objectivist short line and the three-ply line, with positive, enriching consequences for himself and British poetry. Such preoccupation has heightened, not diminished, his essential Englishness; it defines rather than blurs his recognition of otherness. Hence, defining the principle behind *Renga*, the collaborative experiment in four languages with four poets, the "chain of poems" founded on a medieval Japanese poetic form, Jacques Roubaud quotes the fourteenth-century Japanese poet, Shinkei:

The art of renga is not the art of composing poems, or verses of a poem, but a spiritual exercise to penetrate the talent and vision of another.

All the arts are composed only of that which translates from the heart of things into one's own heart.

To follow one's own bent is not the way to experience the indecipherable meaning of others. (34)

The art of translation, therefore, like Tomlinson's contact with American poets and artists, is bound up with his long-standing insistence upon detachment and impersonality, upon the world's otherness, and the subsequent transformation of self. For the benefits are both heightened awareness and what, in an early poem, "The Atlantic," he terms "replenishment." There he describes the four elements – the contrary forces of sun, wind, ocean, and beach – and out of the dialectical scene, ordinary as it is, creates a meaning, a lucidity:

The sun rocks there, as the netted ripple
   Into whose skeins the motion threads it
Glances athwart a bed, honey-combed
   By heaving stones. Neither survives the instant
But is caught back, and leaves, like the after-image
   Released from the floor of a now different mind,
A quick gold, dyeing the uncovering beach

With sunglaze. That which we were,
Confronted by all that we are not,
    Grasps in subservience its replenishment. (*CP* 17)

The wave's motion is caught in the familiar Tomlinson imagery of
thread, but equally familiar and characteristic is the self's "grasp" both
of itself and of the world's otherness, a confrontation which brings not
only "subservience" but "replenishment." The mind may be "a hunter
of forms," as we learned previously (chapter 1), but the illumination it
attains avoids both "vatic lather" and egocentricity. The world itself is
protean, continually weaving new shapes and forms, successfully evading capture, but is made comprehensible by the comprehensive,
copious self of the creative artist. What composers like Schoenberg
reveal is the perpetual translation and replenishment of self and world,
through confrontation of opposites and the recognition of otherness.

Both the replenishment and sense of otherness, gained through relationship and through penetration to the core or centre, constitute
elements in a vision Tomlinson has called "Eden." The term, first
appearing in *Seeing Is Believing* and present still in the latest work, *The
Return*, has been retained throughout, supplemented in *The Shaft* by
another, "Perfections." In "Glass Grain," from *Seeing is Believing* (*CP*
26), the image of "the grain of glass" suggests a likely Blakean influence,
for certainly not only the image but the sense of a Minute Particular is
also present, here and elsewhere in Tomlinson's work. However, while
Tomlinson's Eden requires much the same sense of relation between self
and world found in the Romantic, it is never, given his views on apocalypse, on the same cosmic, apocalyptic scale. His terms are certainly
religious, visionary in character, but his perspective does not extend
beyond the moral to the mystical. His metamorphoses remain anchored
firmly within time and resist transcendence. "I think there's a lack of
myth in my poetry," Tomlinson has said, "because it usually arises
directly from something seen. I want to register *that* in all its clarity or
in all its implications. The nearest I come to myth is that word 'Eden,'
which I can't seem to get rid of and that fits what I'm doing with its
implication of primal things, fresh sensations, direct perceptions
unmuddied."[2] Quoting from his own Notebook, Tomlinson declared in
an epigraph to *Castilian Ilexes*, his "versions" of Antonio Machado, a
preference for "Neither marble hard and everlasting / nor music, painting, / but the word in time." Henry Gifford's description of Machado as

"the poet of temporality"[3] thus applies equally well to his co-translator, Tomlinson, and does not conflict with the latter's Edenic vision. Looking at an imperfection in the glass of a window pane – a glass grain as magnified by the sun shining through on to the wall – he is consequently led to think of parallels, likes, distinctions, and sum totals, in dizzy fugal pattern:

> Think of the fugue's theme:
> After inversions and divisions, doors
> That no keys can open, cornered conceits
> Apprehensions, all ways of knowledge past,
> Eden comes round again, the motive dips
> Back to its shapely self, its naked nature
> Clothed by comparison alone – related.   ("Glass Grain," 26)

The Edenic vision, then, is known within time and the physical world – indeed in the ordinary world we inhabit – and depends upon relationship or "comparison." In *The Shaft*, the section "Perfections" is followed naturally and inevitably by another, "Seasons." Wholeness of perception, moreover, derives from harmony of self, a good Romantic dictum. The various correspondences in the creative perception – whether of subject and object, or senses in a synaesthetic union – are thus paralleled in a further larger unity, which constitutes a vision of Eden.

There are times, however, when the poet insists upon such wholeness while denying the miraculous: in "Under the Moon's Reign" (251) the transformation is achieved

> by no more miracle than the place
>    It occupied and the eye that saw it
> Gathered into the momentary perfection of the scene
>    Under transfigured heavens, under the moon's reign.

On another occasion the Edenic vision comes like a gift, taking the perceiver unawares:

> one instant of morning
> rendered him time
> and opened him space,
> one whole without seam.   ("The Greeting," 260)

More usually it is a vision for which one works, involving a disciplining of both self and senses, a shaping and ordering of self and world, which is the reverse of the coincidental or miraculous. Nevertheless, the religious imagery is maintained and, as we shall see, also the element of chance. Coincidence, after all, means not just chance concurrence but, equally, correspondence, agreement, occupation of the same space. Hence, "At Holwell Farm," as we have seen, reveals that to be "Rooted in more than earth, to dwell / Is to discern the Eden image" (39). It is a quality of being so essential or central that it can be characterized as Edenic, a quality pristine in its newness, yet rooted in origins; clear and unsullied, paradisal, yet never transcendent, and found within time. Likewise, in "Focus," in *American Scenes*, the last of four poems constituting "In Winter Woods" (119–20), the poet describes, in imagery inherited from photography, how "the whole, gigantic / aperture of the day / shuts down to a single / brilliant orifice." The focus is upon another "grain," a green moss glaring up against the stark white of a fallen beech log.

> And the mind
> that swimmer, unabashed
> by season, encounters
> on entering, places
> as intimate as a fire's
> interior palaces: an Eden
> on whose emerald tinder,
> unblinded and unbounded
> from the dominance of white,
> the heart's eye enkindles.

In *The Way of a World*, however, are more substantial poems forming a sequence, later set to music,[4] and providing further, more extended illumination of the Edenic vision. That vision proves, indeed, to be a state of mind more than being; an ideal by which things might be judged, much like his model city or society. The analogy is used in "Eden" (159), perhaps the finest of the group of poems:

> I have seen Eden. It is a light of place
>   As much as the place itself; not a face
> Only, but the expression on that face: the gift

Of forms constellates cliff and stones:
The wind is hurrying the clouds past,
    And the clouds as they flee, ravelling-out
Shadow a salute where the thorn's barb
    Catches the tossed, unroving sack
That echoes their flight. And the same
    Wind stirs in the thicket of the lines
In Eden's wood, the radial avenues
    Of light there, copious enough
To draft a city from.

The several analogies by which Eden is defined indicate the "radial" nature of vision itself. Just as Eden's light radiates outwards in an inclusive, coherent manner, so the analogies the perceiver creates bring together disparate and mutable entities. The flapping of a sack snagged on a thorn corresponds to the clouds hurried across the sky, both sack and clouds given movement by the same wind. In turn, however, the external scene corresponds to the perceiver's internal landscape, where disparate experiences are brought together to form a coherent whole. In the same way, the ideal city is set off against the present, a light of self which illuminates and clarifies but also abhors "This insurrection of sorry roofs." (The image of "insurrection" suitably contradicts and subverts the ideal, ordered society.) And though such enlightenment demands discipline, an ordering of self and world, nevertheless the Edenic remains ultimately a gift, something given rather than earned, like the fortuitousness of rhyme ("The Chances of Rhyme," 194–5). The poem concludes:

There is no
    Bridge but the thread of patience, no way
But the will to wish back Eden, this leaning
    To stand against the persuasions of a wind
That rings with its meaninglessness where it sang its meaning.

The imagery of bridge and thread brings the reader back to the recurrent theme of relationship, but the means by which such relations can be constructed prove fundamentally moral ones – patience and will – and remind us of our need to prepare ourselves for such a gift. In a poem which employs religious imagery to convey aesthetic and epistemological principles, the fact that the wind is attributed "persuasions" (in the sense of religious belief) evidences Tomlinson's fine sense of irony. The wind's several "persuasions" range from "meaninglessness" to the Edenic song of "meaning": from the incoherent perspective, which sees only the mutable character of the temporal flux, to the "radial" coherence of Eden, which depends upon that very mutability for its existence. In the latter, the self, itself ordered and whole, sees by way of analogy and synthesizes the various effects of the wind into a meaning which, while rooted in time and mutability, nevertheless brings illumination of a quasi-religious kind.

On another occasion, the poet, like Adam on the morning of the naming of the beasts, feels "the perpetuity of Eden" ("Adam," 160). In the hands of another poet – say, Ted Hughes – the situation would be given a clear, albeit unorthodox, theological significance. Tomlinson regards it, however, as peculiarly, though not exclusively, aesthetic in nature. Again Octavio Paz proves indispensable: "The experience of art is one of the experiences of Beginning: that archetypal moment in which, combining one set of things with another to produce a new, we reproduce the very moment of the making of the worlds" (*BW* 15). Tomlinson describes it likewise as a "return through materials to origins":

At the centre of Paul Klee's *On Modern Art* stands the passage concerning Genesis, the artist "impressed by the one essential image of creation itself, as Genesis, rather than by the image of nature, the finished product ... He sees the act of world creation stretching from the past to the future. Genesis eternal!"
So Genesis is discovery in the act of making. (20)

In *The Way of a World*, "Adam" is succeeded by "Night Trans- figured" (*CP* 160–1). Its title and nighttime walk acknowledge Schoen- berg in their echo of his string sextet, *Verklärte Nacht*, which in turn is derived from a Richard Dehmel poem about a man and a woman taking such a moonlit walk. Tomlinson's poem substitutes the darkness of night for the brilliance of Adam's day, the "small occurrence" for Adam's momentous occasion, and leads to the poet's awareness of "cenotaph and ceaseless requiem." The occasion and tone are straight- forward and ordinary enough: "Do you recall the night we flung / Our torch-beam down in among / The nettle towers?" Yet the experience provokes a further question, of the night's transfiguration:

What large thing was it stood
   In such small occurrence, that it could
Transfigure the night, as we
   Drew back to find ourselves once more
In the surrounding citadel of height and air?

The poet's answer defines precisely a sense, inarticulated yet certainly experienced by those present, and reaching towards the core of their being and of existence itself. For they come close to time itself and death and, in that proximity of "other," to Eden's transfiguration too. The vision, in other words, brings awareness of all that Eden by definition is not – night, dark, dreadful, and deathlike. Such definition by way of negatives we have seen before; here Tomlinson's lines proceed through successive oxymorons – seeing with words, loud silence, being and non-being, bareness clothed – to ultimate meaning.

   To see then speak, is to see with the words
We did not make. That silence
   Loud with the syllables of the generations, and that sphere
Centred by a millenial eye, all that was not
   There, told us what was, and clothed
The sense, bare as it seemed, in the weave
   Of years: we knew that we were sharers,
Heirs to the commonalty of sight, that the night
   In its reaches and its nearnesses, possessed
A single face, sheer and familiar
   Dear if dread. The dead had distanced,
Patterned its lineaments, and to them
   The living night was cenotaph and ceaseless requiem.

A delicate, delightful, almost playful treatment of the same theme recurs in a later poem, "Juliet's Garden" (229–30), prefaced by an epigraph from Sartre: "J'ai connu une petite fille qui quittait son jardin bruyamment, puis s'en revenait à pas de loup pour 'voir comment il était quand elle n'était pas là.' " The departure of the little girl (the poet's daughter) creates a silence which enables her to experience more acutely both garden and self. For her departure is a "voluntary death"; her non-being heightens, measures, her Eden, defining presence by absence, life by death, infinity by time:[5]

Silently ...
she was quieter than breathing now,
hearing the garden seethe
behind her departed echo:

flowers merely grew,
showing no knowledge of her:
stones hunching their hardnesses
against her not being there:

scents came penetratingly,
rose, apple, and leaf-rot,
earthsmell under them all,
to where she was not:

such presences could only
rouse her fears,
ignoring and perfuming
this voluntary death of hers:

and so she came rushing back
into her garden then,
her new-found lack
the measure of all Eden.

It is a theme to which Tomlinson returns frequently, whether to stress the "medicinal" quality of a northern spring (28) or the sense of "other" and the "shriven self" in "Something: A Direction," the final poem of "Antecedents" (54–5), or to define life as "the daily remaking a body / refleshed of air" ("Dialectic," 223–4). The remaking or resurrection, however, is possible only by knowing what in "Something: A Direction" Tomlinson calls "the textures of your pain." In that poem the poet's language may be abstract, remote from the physical world he usually records vividly, and on occasion reminiscent of Wallace Stevens; on the other hand, the "direction" which the poem points out is one Tomlinson follows in his later work with increased assurance and conviction:

                         Released
     From knowing to acknowledgement, from prison
       To powers, you are new-found

Neighboured, having earned relation
With all that is other. Still you must wait,
  For evening's ashen, like the slow fire
Withdrawn through the whitened log
  Glinting through grain marks where the wood splits:
Let be its being: the scene extends
  Not hope, but the urgency that hopes for means. (54–5)

As we have seen, Tomlinson recognized early that a Stevensian aesthetic possessed several major drawbacks, among the most significant being the solipsism of the self and that self's need to deny the otherness of things. However, he learnt, like Stevens, to consent to time: that endurance of suffering can be a great good, and that evil or pain can be a source of virtue and strength. The Stevensian directive, "Let be its being," is then more than a passive accommodation: it requires, like the little girl's "voluntary death" in "Juliet's Garden," an act of will, a necessary element in the disciplining of the self Tomlinson has persistently upheld. Moreover, the will is most exercised when confronted with pain and suffering. Consequently, in "The Compact: at Volterra" (206–7) he praises man's attempt to order and civilize the chaotic, destructive forces of nature, seemingly in compact against any such attempt. The human will, on the other hand, is stubborn and patient, seeking another kind of "compact," whether of that civic kind (as epitomized in the town) or of the farmers' labour of the land ("They pit their patience against the dust's vacuity"). The result is that "all live / At a truce," recognizing the perennial nature of the struggle and the heroic human endurance and requisite exercise of will. The theme is expressed in a particularly fine early poem, "Harvest Festival: at Ozleworth" (73–4).

At his own Gloucestershire village, the poet is made aware of the ancient, Roman as well as Christian, origins of the harvest festival, and, in Christ's crown of thorns carved in stone in the church chancel arch – a distinctive feature of Ozleworth's church of St Nicholas – a "garland" of a different kind, founded in the greatest agony and heaviest pain, though also the source of rebirth, resurrection, and salvation. Hence, the poet recognizes in the women's arrangements of harvest gifts "The shadow of the old propitiation"; and, in a characteristic correspondence, sees the analogy between that arrangement and the "Leaved capitals" at the heads of the nave's columns. However, both eye and theme are focused by the mason's handiwork in the crown of thorns:

            The chancel arch
     Seemed like the chosen counter-bass
        To show the theme weaving about it. There
     Thorns were the crown to all the fruits: the hand
        That faultlessly had spanned the space, had cut
     For a crossing in the stone, the spines
        Which Christ had worn, long lobes
     In interlacing, shadowed grey.

The setting suitably brings together the various analogues: past and
present, Roman and Christian coincide in a poem heavy with images of
weaving and interlacing; the chancel arch likewise provides yet one
more Tomlinson bridge or span, not just containing a space but filling it
with a distinctive "verdure" (to use the terms of his Schoenberg ode),
with a fruit of thorns, a harvest founded in hurt and suffering but bearing atonement.

                Cruel, these
        Cool fingers, tip to tip, and yet
     Whoever wove them had not lost delight
        In the conception. Though they stood for more
     Than we could ever be or bear, they fed
        The eye with regularity, humanized the hurt.
     This, growing kind, could thus
        Remind us of the necessary pain than none
     Is proof against, and even stone
        Must neighbour.

The hurt's source may lie in man's fallen nature; its transformation into
fruit may in turn depend upon divine creation beyond man; but the
"faultless" spanning of the space through the carving of the crown of
thorns is both an aesthetic and a moral achievement, capable of in-
structing and delighting the eye. The effect upon the perceiver is of
"growing kind" – that is, a growth or enlargement of self which entails
benevolence and affection ("kind") but also that which is appropriate
and pertains to kinship (in two other senses of "kind"). For both these
last two senses bear upon Tomlinson's virtues of propriety, unity, consonance, correspondence, and relationship. Hence the poet's return in
the conclusion to the festival itself, to the conjunction of "delight and

death," of Christ and Ceres, Christian and Roman in this "canon" (in the sense both of law, criterion and exercise of discrimination, and of musical composition). We may remember that Tomlinson early faulted Wallace Stevens on the grounds that he failed to capture that " 'world of canon and fugue,' such as Hopkins spoke of seeing before him" (Author's Preface, *The Necklace*, 1966 ed.). That world is properly and effectively captured and celebrated in "Harvest Festival," as major an early poem in Tomlinson's *oeuvre* as the Schoenberg ode, both poems appearing in the same volume, *A Peopled Landscape* (1963).

Tomlinson's poems in a markedly different setting and culture – in the South-West United States – reveal a similar acceptance of hurt on the part of the Indian and employ that "vocabulary of suffering" which Henry Gifford has ascribed to Machado (*CI* xxi). Regardless of setting, the theme recurs throughout Tomlinson's work as a necessary constituent in his discipline. Occasionally, as in "In the Fullness of Time" (*CP* 163-4), that acceptance is expressed less agonizingly as "our consent to time," a state of mind more easily acquired, as Tomlinson says, when "The unhurried sunset were itself a courtesy." When, however, one is "tied to a dwindling patrimony / And the pain of exile" ("Machiavelli in Exile," 214-15), such consent is less easy. Having as daily companions peasants in place of Borgia princes, Machiavelli "must choose / Such men as endure history and not those / Who make it." In the peasant the will sleeps. For Machiavelli, on the other hand, such exile provides the final discipline, sharpening his vision and creating a style through which he defines the ideal prince:

> Adversity puts his own pen in hand,
> First torture, then neglect bringing to bear
> The style and vigilance which may perfect
> A prince, that he whom history forsook
> Should for no random principle forsake
> Its truth's contingency, his last defeat
> And victory, no battle, but a book.

What Machiavelli achieves is an accommodating vision, reconciling him to exile and suffering without any diminution of pain. Tomlinson describes a similar accommodation in a later volume, *The Way In*, in "The Dream" (*CP* 252-3) and in a fine concluding poem to the same volume, "Melody" (269-70). The final poem is in fact "Da Capo," which reminds us further of the constant repetition and the musical nature of the pattern the poet traces. It is a pattern, as he notes in "Melody," which depends upon dialectical dialogue, "the will / To hear the consequence ... the reply / To 'I am dying, I am denying, I, I. ...' " The fragmentary phrases are suitably egotistic and solipsistic, fusing Cartesian doubt with an awareness of mortality. Consequently, the will generates a contrary phrase, and, in the familiar imagery of violin, river, and thread, creates a music in the self. The narcissistic self-pity is answered, not by any diminution of pain but by "a singing strength":

Until that thread of song, defied,
    Gathering a tributary power, must find
The river course, winding in which
    It can outgo itself – can lose
Not the reality of pain, but that sense
    Of sequestration: the myth of no future
And no ancestry save ache.

Awareness of pain and of the need for endurance can lead to self-pity but also to "sequestration," withdrawal or obtuse acceptance, a living in the present which regards the past as merely pain and denies the possibility of any future difference. The great value of song or melody, on the other hand, is the encompassing of limits, the recognition of pleasure and pain, birth and death, future and past. Correcting Rilke, then, Tomlinson proceeds:

*Gesang*
    *Ist Dasein?* Song is the measure, rather,
Of being's spread and height, the moonrise
    That tips and touches, recovering from the night
The lost hill-lines, the sleeping prospects:
    It is the will to exchange the graph of pain
Acknowledged, charted and repeated, for the range
    Of an unpredicted terrain. Each phrase
Now follows the undulations of slope, rise
    And drop, released along generous contours
And curving towards a sea where
    The play of light across the dark immensity,

Moves in a shimmering completeness. The tide
  Ridden in unexulting quiet, rides
Up against the craft that sails it
  Tossed and tried, through the groundswell
To the dense calm of unfathomable silence.

The self has indeed been "Tossed and tried" but the conclusion is both convincing and moving. The poet has progressed successfully from solipsism and self-pity, through exercise of will and awareness of pain, to possession of that same "measure of being" which characterizes song and which establishes the otherness (the "unpredicted terrain") of the world. Measure, in turn, encompasses both the Edenic vision and "our consent to time" and suffering, the boundaries of Tomlinson's world of event.

# CHAPTER FIVE

# Poetry of Recovery

The common early criticisms levelled against Tomlinson's work – as lacking involvement and humanity, as reflecting abstract, narrow intellectual and aesthetic concerns – are, with hindsight, more easily recognized as misplaced. Clearly from the outset his poetry has been rooted in experience of a vividly physical world. Moreover, as we have seen, Tomlinson's perspectives, landscapes, objects, or mental processes are never ends in themselves. Rather, they serve a purpose beyond both aesthetics and epistemology to constitute what may be called a poetry of recovery; the experiences he charts possess ultimately a moral and social significance. Made even more acutely aware of time's destructive character in a century of demolition and disintegration, he seeks to conserve, to maintain balance, to shape order out of chaos, to achieve relationship within the self, amongst one's fellow men, and with the world. Relationship, for Tomlinson, involves active participation, a dynamic exchange or negotiation, but it also requires detachment, impersonality, and, above all, an acknowledgment of otherness, whether of the physical world or of other selves. At the same time his world is one of event rather than spectacle; his perspectives draw not just the eye but the whole self into relationship, into vision unified and real.

While much of Tomlinson's work may rightly be characterized as contemplative, analytical of the act of perception and one's experience of the world, it has never excluded other people. As if to answer his first critics, the very title of his third volume, *A Peopled Landscape*, was explicit; the landscape is populated, indeed, by John Mayhew, Mrs Spaxton, the farmer's wife, Elizabeth Grieve, the farmhand, and his own daughter J.T. Likewise, of that volume he wrote, somewhat defensively but nevertheless accurately, in rebuttal of his critics:

In my last volume, *Seeing Is Believing*, humanity was present by implication in the buildings, landscapes and artefacts contained in the poems and there was, of course, the human mind of the poet as it dealt with these impingements. In *A Peopled Landscape* there are both animals and people, perhaps more numerously than before, and I was glad when in "Over Brooklyn Bridge" I was able to persuade one of my characters to talk with a voice not my own.[1]

His poetry of recovery seeks not just the judicious shaping and recollection of experience in a dynamic exchange of self and world but, as another form of that exchange, communication between people, a poetry of the speaking voice. A year later, in 1964, in conversation with Ian Hamilton, he indicated even more explicitly the true direction of his poetry, towards relationship with both the physical world and people, relationship which acknowledges their otherness:

The terms on which I write about things are the same terms on which true relationship with people becomes possible; that's to say, in my "thing" poems, there is a sense of letting the other be, a containment of self, if you like. Also, a lot of things I write about – houses, cities, walls, landscapes – are so saturated in human presence and traditions that to consciously introduce "people" would be pointless. On the other hand, some of my best things – "Up at La Serra" for example – begin and end with people.[2]

However, acknowledgment of the otherness of both people and things does not preclude – on the contrary, it permits – communication. A decade later he admitted that his poems frequently addressed a reader: "I do always feel I'm speaking to someone." Indeed, his poet, after Wordsworth, an increasingly valid parallel, is "a man speaking to men."[3]

For the most part Tomlinson's critics have attended too exclusively to his philosophical concerns and not listened to his poetic voice. While the visual character of his work is obvious and central, the effect sought depends also upon the ear, upon the poet's use of tone, cadence, and diction. His voice is frequently wry, ironic, and witty, and his sense of comedy, like his capacity for feeling, has been seriously underestimated. His increasing mastery of lineation, of the short line inherited from modern American poetry, is used partly to convey colloquial rhythms and everyday speech but also to gain witty effects. While seeking Wordsworth's "real language of men," he learnt early and practically from Marianne Moore and William Carlos Williams. He praised Moore, for example, for doing what Chaucer and Wyatt did for writing in their day – namely, making "available to verse the materials and cadences of prose speech and prose writing."[4] Moreover, the three-ply line contributes to what elsewhere he has called "letting the look of the poem on the page prompt and regulate *through the eye* the precise tone of the voice."[5] Again, he directed the readers of *A Peopled Landscape* thus: "the short lines of these poems are not to be read *staccato*: they are intended to be full of the *rubato* of daily speech, to be kept in flowing movement like a melody and, like a melody, to be felt out against their accompanying silence."[6] We might expect by this time such a musical analogy and terms, and while other British poets of the period like Larkin strove similarly to capture "the *rubato* of daily speech," Tomlinson found help from a source Larkin deliberately set his face against, from modern American poetry.

Consequently, he praised the distinctive achievement of a William Carlos Williams poem, an achievement, he noted, which readers on both sides of the Atlantic failed at first to recognize:

how its recovery of weight in the syllabic components (a term like "free verse" does little to account for this) brings a new care into both music and syntax. It is only in the fifties and sixties ... that attention has moved in this direction and that such poetry begins to be seen, as in Robert Duncan's "Notes on Poetics" in its fuller implications for other poets – and not merely American ones.[7]

Tomlinson practised such art himself in a "Letter to Dr. Williams," first published in 1957, not included in his individual volumes or in the *Collected Poems*. Yet the English poet acknowledges the vital contribution of Williams to the very three-ply cadence he takes over, a cadence significantly related not just to voice but to similarly crucial Tomlinson concerns, space and the poet's articulation of space through time ("cadence"):

                    We have gained

    a world, and you
                have enlivened a discipline
                        by a propriety of cadence

that will pass

> into the common idiom
>> like the space

of Juan Gris

> and Picasso –
>> invented to be of use

and for the rearticulation
> of inarticulate facts.[8]

Even when not employing such a line, as in "A Garland for Thomas Eakins" (*CP* 139–42), Tomlinson makes the nineteenth-century American artist come alive by way of his *obiter dicta*:

> – And what do you think of
> that, Mr. Eakins? (A Whistler)
> – I think that that
> is a very cowardly way to paint.

Other poems, such as "Mr. Brodsky," which wittily describes the Tomlinsons' bagpipe-playing neighbour in Albuquerque, or "News from Nowhere" (*America West South West*), which puts into verse a Mark Twain letter,[9] or "Class," which ruthlessly castigates British class prejudices towards particular accents – all capture voice and character through rhythm and syntax. Indeed, he manages the same effect when he incorporates fragments of Spanish into his New Mexican poems (as in "Las Trampas U.S.A.," *CP* 124). For in capturing another's distinctive voice or character or language, the poet is also, like a good translator, acknowledging otherness. At the same time, his critics are not wholly at fault: for all their use of the speaking voice, these remain for the most part less substantial, less satisfying Tomlinson poems.

More substantial, central to his achievement and increasingly employing a speaking voice are Tomlinson's reflective lyrics, a form appropriate to his recurrent meditation upon experiences and to the neo-Augustan quality which Donald Davie early attributed to him. Tomlinson's use of the reflective lyric, however, is derived less from Augustan models like Gray's "Elegy on a Country Churchyard" or

Goldsmith's "The Deserted Village" than from Wordsworth and, above all, from Coleridge. Indeed, Coleridge's presence in *The Return* is considerable: "From Porlock" focuses upon the fateful intrusion of the business visitor from Porlock upon the Romantic poet dreaming of Kubla Khan, while other poems are indebted to Coleridge's conversation poems. It is in the latter that interior and external landscapes fuse, that the mind's dialectical patterns are pursued, and that reflection is expressed in a fluency close to good conversation, albeit often with one's self. And while we may find reflective lyrics early in Tomlinson's work, the distinctively Coleridgean parallel is a later development, as is the increased fluency. Compare the greater formality of tone, diction and syntax in these lines from "The Mausoleum" (25) –

> Were I a guide you would vouchsafe my legend
>     Of how a race halted in tumult here
> To exorcise in such a wavering light
>     The authority of death

– with the conversational fluency and immediacy of everyday occurrence in "Night Transfigured" (160) published eleven years later:

> Do you recall the night we flung
>     Our torch-beam down in among
> The nettle towers?

Perhaps not coincidentally, Tomlinson's finer reflective lyrics in the volumes of the last fifteen years have often depended on the presence of others or awareness of their absence and on their colloquy direct and indirect, spoken or unspoken – "Hillwalk" (257), "Departure" (289), "The Flood" (346–8), and two poems from his latest volume, *The Return*, the title poem and the loving tribute to his wife, "Winter Journey" (*Return* 33–5).

The last, divided into four sections, traces the poet's separation from his wife, who must journey some distance through a wintry landscape, their communication during her absence, and his preparations for her return. Several details suggest parallels with two major Coleridge conversation poems, "This Lime-Tree Bower My Prison" and "Frost at Midnight," whether the acutely felt separation from loved ones, settings of wintry nighttime landscape and domestic hearth, threats to safety and happiness provoking anxiety and fear, communication through feeling and relationship, or, with the return and a circle completed, the sense of wholeness restored. For just as Coleridge in "This Lime-Tree Bower" imagines his friends' progress through a landscape, so, similarly motivated by love, Tomlinson follows his wife's journey: "I was dreaming your way for you, my dear, / Freed of the mist that followed the snow here" (with echoes also of "The Ancient Mariner"); "I saw a scene climb up all around you"; "My eye took in / Close-to, among the vastnesses you passed unharmed, / The shapes the frozen haze hung on the furze / Like scattered necklaces." His wife's letter brings news of her safety and so reassurance, but also transforms threat to shared "images of beauty." The transformation, like all such experiences in Tomlinson, depends upon relationship and its concrete expression, touch. Their correspondence (letter) entails sharing a common dream, another form of correspondence, touchingly caught.

> It must have been
> The firm prints of your midnight pen
>    Over my fantasia of snow, told you were safe,
> Turning the threats from near and far
>    To images of beauty we might share
> As we shared my dream that now
>    Flowed to the guiding motion of your hand,
> As though through the silence of propitious dark
>    It had reached out to touch me across sleeping England.

In his wife's absence the poet, like Coleridge, turns to past shared experience – "Alone in the house, I thought back to our flood" – and through attending to the stream's present sound is led to think "Of consequence and distance." For "consequence" signifies variously the stream's potential for flood, its constant movement or course, its importance as well as its musical sequence. But the distance separating poet and wife is also of profound personal consequence to them both, bringing threat and potential loss but also heightened perception and intensified harmony. Whether the rhyming of ear and stream or husband and wife, "The truce that distils note-perfect out of dusk" is to be celebrated. At the same time the poet recognizes that such harmony born out of flux remains inevitably subject to that flux. Equally, the moon's clarity acknowledged in the third section leads to recognition of the poet's ignorance and aloneness amidst the night sky's immensity. Yet such clarity is seen also more positively as "Burning and burgeoning against your return."

The poem's final section not only details the husband's preparations for his wife's return – "I lay the table where, tonight, we eat," "I uncork the wine. I pile the hearth" – but again points to the external world of sun, day, twilight, nighttime, as if that world participates sympathetically with the poet in enabling his wife's safe return.

> The sun, as it comes indoors out of space
> Has left a rainbow irising each glass –
>   A refraction, caught then multiplied
> From the crystal tied within our window,
>   Threaded up to transmit the play
> And variety day deals us. By night
>   The facets take our flames into their jewel
> That, constant in itself, burns fuelled by change
>   And now that the twilight has begun
> Lets through one slivered shaft of reddening sun.

The same clarity of vision has enabled him to distinguish the stream's music and the moon's clarity; the prismatic nature of experience, whether through refraction, crystal, facets, or the thread imagery, Tomlinson has caught precisely from the outset. Now, however, clarity and precision are accompanied by a warmth of feeling, an intimate expression of self not out of keeping with the reflective character of his lyric.

> I uncork the wine. I pile the hearth
> With the green quick-burning wood that feeds
>   Our winter fires, and kindle it
> To quicken your return when dwindling day
>   Must yield to the lights that beam you in
> And the circle hurry to complete itself where you began,
>   The smell of distance entering with the air,
> Your cold cheek warming to the firelight here.

As Donne, a Tomlinson master, attests in "A Valediction: Forbidding Mourning," also through imagery of the circle's completion, such inti-

mate relationship is made possible through refraction, such completeness achieved through change, separation, distance as well as return.
The poem thus testifies to the essential nature of touch, of correspondence and relationship, while at the same time offering a touching testa-
ment of love.

"Winter Journey" reveals Tomlinson's use of the reflective lyric to
express a warmth and intimacy his critics have too frequently denied
him. Indeed, the superbly ironic portrait of Descartes in an earlier
poem, "Descartes and the Stove" (*CP* 166–7), succeeds largely through
another quality critics have been slow to recognize – that "element of
epistemological comedy" Tomlinson has claimed for "very many" of
his poems.[10] Here the philosopher's subjective experiences are used in
gentle refutation of his metaphysics, so that we are treated to a picture
of Descartes's famous stove, threatening to "melt" the philosopher "into
recognition":

> Thrusting its armoury of hot delight,
>     Its negroid belly at him, how the whole
> Contraption threatened to melt him
>     Into recognition. Outside, the snow
> Starkened all that snow was not –
>     The boughs' nerve-net, angles and gables
> Denting the brilliant hoods of it.

Once more definition is gained through perception of its negative – "the
snow / Starkened all that snow was not" – the very verb "Starkened"
capturing the effect of definition while also resisting any blurring of
feeling as well as of sight. The poet's eye is thus drawn, in un-Cartesian
immediacy, to the effect of declining light upon the wintry landscape.

>                     Now
> The last blaze of day was changing
>     All white to yellow, filling
> With bluish shade the slots and spoors
>     Where, once again, badger and fox would wind
> Through the phosphorescence.

As night descends, reducing such starkly highlighted brilliance to
"anonymity" and darkness, the focus shifts inside to the famous
philosopher:

     The great mind
Sat with his back to the unreasoning wind
   And doubted, doubted at his ear
The patter of ash and, beyond, the snow-bound farms,
   Flora of flame and iron contingency
And the moist reciprocation of his palms.

The Cartesian methodological doubt is caught marvellously with the impedance, then acceleration of rhythm achieved by the simple repetition, "doubted, doubted." Moreover, the famous method of reasoning is set off against "the unreasoning wind," the ash falling from the stove, even Descartes's sweating hands. For his palms "reciprocate" in a way his intellect fails to do concerning the existence of an external material world. In addition, the flow of imagery in the last lines – from the philosopher's room, back, and ear, the stove's ash, to the outside world of snow, farms, and back to the flame, stove, and sticky palms – radiates outwards and returns, suggesting precisely that "reciprocation" of self and world "the great mind" is doubting. It is indeed a "contingency" – of things coming together and by chance. Such a double meaning is deliberately chosen, because, as Tomlinson stresses increasingly, such correspondence of self and world is given and not arrived at by way of methodologies, Cartesian or otherwise. Consequently, the incongruity of doubting mind, "unreasoning wind," and, above all, that "moist reciprocation of his palms," provides witty and effective proof of the material world, if not for Descartes, then certainly for both poet and reader.

   The presence of people in Tomlinson's poetry depends, however, less upon the need to silence critical objection and more upon his longstanding wish to unite verse and the speaking voice, and so effect a revitalized language for poetry. At the same time his people serve thematic as well as technical ends, expressing, as in the portrait of Descartes, the poet's central and lasting concerns. What is striking about the figures in his later landscapes is that they reveal, more so than previously, not only the moral and social relevance but the conservative and preservationist spirit of his poetry. The people, childhood experiences, and landscapes of The Way In enable him to seek a way into his own past, into the single landscape primary to all his experiences ("At Stoke," 243), a landscape both industrial and internal. The society proves mindless, indifferent to the ugliness and scarring of land

and eye, careless in what it demolishes and vulgar in what it substitutes. The old couple pushing the rag cart in the volume's title poem thus become near-allegorical figures, the woman first "a sexagenarian Eve," then "mindless Mnemosyne":[11]

> She is our lady of the nameless metals, of things
>   No hand has made, and no machine
> Has cut to a nicety that takes the mark
>   Of clean intention – at best, the guardian
> Of all that our daily contact stales and fades,
>   Rusty cages and lampless lampshades. (242)

The poet is in search of a "civility" he fails to find: "It will need more than talk and trees / To coax a style from these disparities."

The "mindless Mnemosyne" figure in "The Way In" epitomizes a fearful mechanization and dehumanization to which Tomlinson objects strenuously, but which characterize the age. In the previous volume, *Written on Water*, driving through a landscape allowed different, positive perspectives, creating new possibilities, new angles, ever-changing lights and shades. In *The Way In*, the car becomes a destructive force, seen much as D.H. Lawrence characterized it in the 1920s. Tomlinson's anger and sense of loss – of civility and relationship, and of particular landmarks – are directed there at the demolition of parts of Bristol, brought down in the name of progress and in the service of speed. With his own foot on the accelerator, the poet shares responsibility; indeed, by his movement through traffic he is reminded of the same flux to which all things are subject. Hence, seeing the local population as "A race in transit, a nomad hierarchy," the poet feels "a daily discontent" in his struggle to preserve and create order out of chaos. The problem is at the heart of his poetry of recovery and touches upon a related concern, place:

the desolation of our own urban landscape has produced no place at all, and the way into my book [*The Way In*] lies through such a stretch of unfeatured surroundings. No name could stick to them. They are the barren outward sign of that mixture of avarice and callous utopianism which robs us of place and places today.

As my poetry is a poetry of contemplation, so it is a poetry of returns to objects and to scenes long looked at and consulted for images of relationship and habitation.[12]

The comment pertains to *The Way In* but is relevant to Tomlinson's work as a whole; his most recent volume is *The Return*, in which he returns to places which early provoked his imagination. He has been motivated consistently by a strong Lawrencean sense of place and of the relationship which should necessarily exist between man and landscape. Further, while the growth of the self derives more particularly from its participation in and awareness of time and flux, Tomlinson has also been drawn to that which withholds time, sets limits, contains, shapes order. His containment of self is a similar establishment of limits, of passion and ego, as well as a recognition of the other. His poetry of recovery is firmly based in the striving for rootedness in a world peculiarly destructive of such stabilities.

*The Way In* may contain a larger than usual number of poems directed against the blight of a landscape, the demolition of cities, the bad taste of much modern architecture, or the sorry consequences of myopic town planning. But Tomlinson has never overlooked the industrial scene and has maintained a constant campaign against mindless destruction and ugliness. An early poem, "On the Hall at Stowey," in *Seeing Is Believing* (CP 40–2), for example, contrasts unfavourably the pride and patience epitomized by the Hall and "Our prodigal time." Indifferent now to what the Hall represents, we have abandoned it to time and the natural elements, though not before

> Each hearth refitted
> For a suburban whim, each room
> Denied what it was, diminished thus
> To a barbarous mean, had comforted (but for a time)
> Its latest tenant.

Of the present, the poet can only add, "What we had not / Made ugly, we had laid waste." A similar barbarous vandalism is highlighted in several other poems, particularly in *The Way In* and *The Shaft*. "Waste / Is our way," as he declares in one ("Casarola," 286), although adding in this instance of a neglected rural landscape that "There is a beauty / In this abandonment." Like Larkin in "Going, Going," Tomlinson was commissioned to write a poem (in his case for the Shakespeare Birthplace Trust) and, like Larkin, he proceeded to attack contemporary ugliness and vulgarity:

> Arden is not Eden, but Eden's rhyme:
>  Time spent in Arden is time at risk
> And place, also: for Arden lies under threat:
>  Ownership will get what it can for Arden's trees:
> No acreage of green-belt complacencies
>  Can keep Macadam out:   ("In Arden," 305)

Tomlinson has persistently attacked bad taste, vulgarity, ugliness, and squalor wherever they are found – whether in the "garishness" of "A Navajo blanket / woven in a Lancashire factory" (86); in "our neo-New Mexican parlour" (128); on an Indian reservation-turned-motel (128–32); or, a British equivalent, "Where an ice cream van circulates the estate / Playing Greensleeves" (157). In all these instances the poet is motivated by a desire to preserve good taste, discrimination, moderation, rationality, elegance – qualities to be ranged with his Yeatsian preference for ceremony. Instead of Romantic quests for discovery, the poet proclaims, "I want the voyage of recovery" (233).

Seeking more than mere conservation, however, he directs us towards that moral sense which comes whether from striving for order against chaos or from choosing beauty above ugliness. Such a moral sense extends towards relationship, between an individual and the external world, between individuals themselves, and between people generally in the larger framework of society. The impulse once again is in part classical, Augustan, away from the worst forms of Romanticism – excess, egotism, and subjectivism – towards civility, civic relations, civilized exchanges, at the heart of which lies proper respect for the individual and the particular. Respecting both language and society, Tomlinson has thus objected to political poetry, particularly for "that very ugly and inflated rhetoric that mistakes itself for poetry when all it is doing is enjoying a bath in its own righteous indignation."[13] Yet, for all his apparent Augustanism, Tomlinson remains intrinsically within the Romantic tradition of self-fulfilment, his model Wordsworth rather than Blake. He may have begun writing in imitation of Blake and Whitman, but his poetry of recovery, in which recollection is crucial, has more in common with Wordsworth than Blake, for whom memory was distinguished from the daughters of Inspiration (*A Vision of the Last*

*Judgment*.) Likewise, his conservatism, whether of experience or of society and politics, more closely matches that of Wordsworth than the revolutionary program of a Blake.

A natural corollary to Tomlinson's poetry of recovery and concern for civility is his preoccupation with history and the pastness of things. Yet once again he avoids Romantic excess. "History," he has declared, "is ... an arc that resists completion, though men are always trying to fix it through revolution or mystical transcendence. I see the assassination of Trotsky in *The Way of a World* ["Assassin"] as an attempt to transcend time, almost as a caricature of mysticism, an attempt to have the future *now* on one's own terms and the result of trying to complete *that* circle is inhumanity."[14] Time indeed has been a constant antagonist, displaying contrary aspects, like Blake's God, prolifically creative and devastatingly destructive. Moreover, as the poet himself grows older, the subject of death in the later volumes has become more prominent and personally relevant. "We cannot climb these slopes without our dead," as he declares in the title poem of his latest volume, *The Return* (10). In a fine early poem, "The Churchyard Wall" (*CP* 55-6), the dead in their "silent community of graves" judge the modern mason, ranging past against present values. They represent the finitude of things, whether men or walls, while the craftsmanship put into the construction of the churchyard wall serves to protect both living and dead. The masons' contribution to the village or town is unacknowledged but none the less considerable – the point, like the poem's subject, has a Wordsworthian quality to it.

> They leave completed
>    Their intent and useful labours to be ignored,
>  To pass into common life, a particle
>    Of the unacknowledged sustenance of the eye,
>  Less serviceable than a house, but in a world of houses
>    A merciful structure. The wall awaits decay.

Man needs such merciful structures, offering protection to both the sleeping dead and the knot of talkers gathering in the sun. In the last resort, all in the landscape are subject to the same decaying process, but the impulse to provide protection for the community reflects that which the poet fails to find elsewhere – for example, in American ghost towns – namely, the "human / meanings, human need" (134). Rather, society brings definition as well as security to human life, a setting of limits or boundaries like the churchyard wall. So too do all things in their otherness:

At the edge of conversations, uncompleting all acts of thought, looms the insistence of things which, waiting on our recognition, face us with our own death, for they are so completely what we are not. And thus we go on trying to read them, as if they were signs, or the embodied message of oracles. We remember how Orpheus drew voices from the stones.     ("The Insistence of Things," 260)

A similar "recognition" is achieved in "After a Death," a finely felt poem (253–4), in which a person's death is seen against the landscape and vista of a clear blue winter sky. Just as "This burial place straddles a green hill" giving distance and meaning to the town below, so too the poet seeks "a sense to read the whole / Reverted side of things," gaining "That height and prospect such as music brings – / Music or memory." The blue January sky, with its "moonshell" imaging the life-death process, is both "that blaze, that blade," providing a destructiveness before which verse is inadequate. But as the poet reads aloud the verse on the gravestone, the words spoken shape the space and provide "An earnest" or foretaste of our eventual loss of breath. The familiar Romantic temptations of transcendence and evasion, however, are firmly resisted ("To live forever, or to cease to live") and, in the impartiality of the light, cleansing what are seen as the town's "wounds," the poet finds "assuagement."

Words,
Bringing that space to bear, that air
   Into each syllable we speak, bringing
An earnest to us of the portion
   We must inherit, what thought of that would give
The greater share of comfort, greater fear –
   To live forever, or to cease to live?
The imageless unnaming upper blue
   Defines a world, all images
Of endeavours uncompleted. Torn levels
   Of the land drop, street by street,
Pitted and pooled, its wounds
   Cleansed by a light, dealt out

With such impartiality you'd call it kindness,
   Blindly assuaging where assuagement goes unfelt. (254)

The assuagement given by the light's impartiality is somewhat like the effect upon the village of the rebuilt churchyard wall – both provide a sustenance, not consciously experienced but none the less real for all that. A more conscious effect would belong to that brand of Romanticism which the poet seeks to avoid.

Man builds walls or cities, then, for protection and security but also, and equally important, for definition. A wall or any other "civic" structure establishes relationships within both time and space, between man and nature, amongst man's fellows. Tomlinson's later volumes – particularly *The Way In*, *The Shaft*, and *The Flood* – express the powerful agency of time and history, together with another recurrent concern, the moral necessity of human society and civilities. In memory, at least, time is suspended, which partly explains the emphasis the poet gives in *The Way In* to his return to the Midlands and his childhood. The poems are rooted in his personal past and its definition through dates: "Nineteen-thirty, our window had for view / The biggest gasometer in England. / Time, no doubt, has robbed that record, too" ("Etruria Vale," 243–4); "It was the place to go in nineteen-thirty, / And so we went" ("Gladstone Street," 244–5); or again:

It was new about eighteen-sixty.
Eighteen-sixty had come to stay, and did
Until the war – the second war, I mean.
Wasn't forty-five our nineteen-seventeen –
The revolution we had all of us earned?   ("Dates: Penkhull New Road," 245)

Place as well as time is important, and walls again play their part: "A race of gardeners died, and a generation / Hacked down the walls to park their cars / Where the flowers once were" (244); or "the other side" of the street

                  – the side
I envied, because its back-yards ran sheer
To the factory wall, warm, black, pulsating,
A long, comforting brick beast. (245)

Moreover, the poet himself admits to a previous aestheticism, over-come only by time and the need to preserve:

> It took time to convince me that I cared
> For more than beauty: I write to rescue
> What is no longer there – absurd
> A place should be more fragile than a book. (245)

And indeed it does "take time" – not just time's passing but the very medium, time itself, making possible that recognition or insight into the nature of things which lies at the heart of Tomlinson's vision. As we saw earlier, temporal flux and distance heightened relationship between poet and wife in "Winter Journey." It may be that in *The Necklace* he practised too exclusive an aestheticism. Yet since at least his second volume, *Seeing Is Believing*, he has "cared / For more than beauty," defining time and place, shaping the self and its experiences, preserving whatever possesses clarity or stability or civility. A poem thus becomes "this house of vocables" (*A* 29), defining time, space, and the creative self. Likewise, his landscapes, while retaining their otherness, are also constructions of mind and eye, not passively perceived but organized into relation: "Place is the focus," he declared early ("In Defence of Metaphysics," *CP* 37); a structure like a house is "a hub / For the scat-tered deployment" ("Northern Spring," 28), providing definition not only for the eye but for the moral sense.

Walls, houses, architecture, poems, style, measure, aesthetic crea-tions – all preserve, define, and so bring enlightenment of self, growth of one's moral consciousness. Yet for all his poetry of recovery, Tom-linson seeks that enlightenment and growth within the existential condi-tion itself. Such is the subject of another fine reflective lyric, "Hill Walk" (257–8). The poem illustrates the fluency with which Tomlinson can inherit the Romantic clichés – the journey through a landscape; the seasonal ambivalence of April; man and nature; the abyss – and still offer his distinctive vision. The poem begins with the familiar Tomlin-son chillness of air, a constant condition for heightened distinctness and definition. The foreign lineaments of Provence and its flowers reinforce these disparities, sharpening both sense and memory.

> Innumerable and unnameable, foreign flowers
> Of a reluctant April climbed the slopes

Beside us. Among them, rosemary and thyme
　　Assuaged the coldness of the air, their fragrance
So intense, it seemed as if the thought
　　Of that day's rarity had sharpened sense, as now
It sharpens memory. And yet such pungencies
　　Are there an affair of every day – Provençal
Commonplaces, like the walls, recalling
　　In their broken sinuousness, our own
Limestone barriers, half undone
　　By time, and patched against its sure effacement
To retain the lineaments of a place.
　　In our walk, time used us well that rhymed
With its own herbs.

Time's rhymes, however, are of various kinds: the obvious homony-
mic time/thyme, certainly, but also the "rhyming" contact of walkers
and their "sharpened sense" with flowers and landscape; of the day in
the poet's sharpened memory, and thus of time itself; of Provençal
walls and the poet's English limestone ones, also subject to time and "its
sure effacement." Walls hold a particular fascination for Tomlinson, as
we have seen: they delineate, contain, withhold, functioning much as
does the shaping creative self or a poetry of recovery. Here they "retain
the lineaments of a place" – the Blakean term indicates the inheritance
of an early exemplar. However, not the least is one more "rhyming,"
that of poet and friends – the poem is dedicated to Philippe and Anne-
Marie Jaccottet – a correspondence without sentimentality or effusion,
but real and warm, none the less. (Indeed, the relationship between
friends is a crucial and recurrent theme for Tomlinson, providing a
"palpable" reality as the climax to *Airborn* and giving the lie to the
objection that he is cold, impersonal, and remote. Wholly characteristic, therefore, is his imaging elsewhere the numinous moment as "a
perfect neighbouring" [289–90].) Here, in "Hill Walk," with the plateau
gained, the walkers can look back over the landscape traversed,
measuring distance and achievement. Again, in proper Tomlinson
fashion, the citadel facing them seems "unseizable," although neither
assault nor victory is contemplated. Instead of such Romantic notions,
the poet prefers "Fragility," which "seemed sufficiency," acknowledging both human limitations and time's perpetual and inevitable
progress.

All stretched to the first fold
Of that unending landscape where we trace
　　Through circuits, drops and terraces
The outworks, ruinous and outgrown,
　　Where space on space has labyrinthed past time:
The unseizable citadel glimmering back at us,
　　We contemplated no assault, no easy victory:
Fragility seemed sufficiency that day
　　Where we sat by the abyss, and saw each hill
Crowned with its habitations and its crumbled stronghold
　　In the scents of inconstant April, in its cold.

Whatever the Romantic clichés of the day's walk, the nature of the experience has been quite the opposite: the poet has been reminded of the need for resistance and otherness, not absorption; for relationship with detachment; for rhyme, but also definition and disparities. And his conclusion likewise prefers the sense of flux to any unreal or extravagant claims for man. The abyss is present, like the citadel, but the chillness of air is matched by a similar keenness of perception, detachment of self and moral awareness, on the poet's part, qualities which prove more satisfying indeed than misguided Romanticism. Any likely decline of recovery into mere nostalgia is thus halted by the poet's fine sense of "Fragility" – a potential weakness is thus turned into a strength.

Such an illumination of self through rhyme or "neighbouring" depends, however, upon yet another conjunction – of choice and chance – that which most defines man and that which most characterizes the unknowable and uncontrollable world of other. Previous poets, like Hardy or Yeats, have been drawn to that same conjunction of choice and chance, although Tomlinson has been made more acutely aware of the conjunction's necessary nature through his experiences both as a painter discovering his technical breakthrough in 1970 with the help of Oscar Domínguez's decalcomania, and as a collaborator in the previous year in the collective composition of *Renga*. For example, among "the affinities and analogies between the games of the surrealists and the renga," Octavio Paz includes the element of chance: "In both, the intrusion of chance is a condition of the game, but the rules which originate the game are distinct and even opposed. With the surrealists, chance works in an open space: the passivity of critical consciousness ... In the renga, chance works as one of the signs of the game ... Chance does not appear in a free space but on the track laid down by the rules" (*Renga* 20). Likewise, Tomlinson asks of the artist's apparently chance discovery, "what is chance? And if one accepts it, does it not cease to be chance?" (*Eden* 15). Yet he proceeds to refer to the influence upon his own painting of surrealism, particularly that of Domínguez. For his own chance discovery in the seventies provoked a period of intense activity which, regrettably, has now ceased.

The element of chance that helped resolve my problems as a painter was the surrealist device known as decalcomania. Briefly, the recipe for this is the one drawn up by Oscar Domínguez in 1936: "By means of a thick brush, spread out black gouache more or less diluted in places, upon a sheet of glossy white paper, and cover at once with a second sheet, upon which exert an even pressure. Lift off the second sheet without haste." Well, the result of this process, as the pigment separates out into random patterns, can be a lot of wasted paper, occasionally a very beautiful entire image, sometimes interesting fragments that prompt and defy the imagination to compose them into a picture. You can alter what is given with a brush, or you can both alter and recombine your images by going to work with scissors and paste and making a collage. The weakness of this technique is that it can lead to a flaccid fantasy of imaginary animals, or of lions turning into bicycles. Its strength lies in its challenge to mental sets, in the very impersonality of the material offered you and that you must respond to. A very unCézannian undertaking, and yet what I have called the ethic of Cézanne – submission to the given, the desire to break with preconceived images of the given, the desire to seize on and stabilize momentary appearances – this ethic, once applied, can lead your decalcomania away from the arbitrariness of fantasy towards the threshold of new perceptions.               (*Eden* 15–16)

The "threshold" brought not "fantasy," then, but a "rhyming" of experience and reunion of artistic functions: "I saw black become dazzling: I saw  the shimmer of water, light and air take over from the merely fortuitous: I saw that I was working now as poet *and* painter once more" (16). Moreover, while that period ended in early 1979, Tomlinson notes a "sufficiency" – the same term used previously in "Hill Walk":

Those ten years, when I was working as poet and painter, possessed a strange radiating sufficiency, both for the large quantity of graphic work I was enabled to produce, and for the effect this had on my writing – namely, of admitting into it a greater regard for chance and for the mysterious fulness of the given. Though I have ceased to make pictures I feel that my poems still lie open to forces emanating from that now completed phase. It seems, in retrospect, to have been like a season in Eden. (73)

Concerning those same collages, Octavio Paz has asked pertinently:

Has it all been a product of chance? But what is meant by that word? Chance is never produced by chance. Chance possesses a logic – is a logic. Because we have yet to discover the rules of something, we have no reason to doubt that there are rules. (*BW* 13)

"What we call chance is nothing but the sudden revelation of relation-ships between things. Chance is an aspect of analogy" (Paz, *BW* 14). Moreover, in praising the decalcomania of another surrealist, Max Ernst, Tomlinson has stressed the active element of choice within chance itself: "Constable waited upon chance, Ernst created it" (21). Hence, in a later poem, "Rhymes" (*CP* 290), "the eye's command" and "the coping hand" combine to create an experience of perfection in which "Word and world rhyme." Yet just as the rhyme, word/world, is imperfect because incomplete, so too is man's knowledge of perfection. It is a moment, as Tomlinson insists in "The Perfection" (290–1), of which we become aware only after it has already gone. Yet our experi-ence of it at all is the result of the rhyme of choice and chance.

In a superb prose poem, "Skullshapes" (191), the poet, as we might now expect, describes not so much the skulls themselves as his percep-tion of them, defining clearly the dynamic process of perception. But the "possibility" of which he talks is precisely the fortuitousness of rhyme, whether amongst words, perceptions, people, places, or instances.

One sees. But not merely the passive mirrorings of the retinal mosaic – nor, like Ruskin's blind man struck suddenly by vision, without memory or conception. The senses, reminded by other seeings, bring to bear on the act of vision their pattern of images; they give point and place to an otherwise naked and home-less impression. It is the mind sees. But what it sees consists not solely of that by which it is confronted grasped in the light of that which it remembers. It sees possibility.

In "seeing," the mind creates a structure for what previously had been simply "homeless"; it defines, like a wall or house. Moreover, he promoted the same "possibility" and essential humanity earlier in "A Meditation on John Constable" (33–5). And although in that poem he argued "The artist lies / For the improvement of truth" and has continued to uphold the moral dimension of his own art, he remains as opposed to mere didacticism as to Romantic apocalypse:

> What is it for? Answers
> should be prepaid. And no Declines
> of the West Full Stop
> No selling lines.   ("Ars Poetica," 222)

The "possibility" which "the mind sees" derives from the creative coincidence of chance, a rhyme of self and world, to the exclusion of Romantic excess. The process is defined wittily and precisely in "The Chances of Rhyme" (194–5):

> The chances of rhyme are like the chances of meeting –
>     In the finding fortuitous, but once found, binding:
> They say, they signify and they succeed, where to succeed
>     Means not success, but a way forward
> If unmapped, a literal, not a royal succession;
>     Though royal (it may be) is the adjective or region
> That we, nature's royalty, are led into.

Art is no more "all form" than life "all Sturm-und-Drang"; and to Crewe or Mow Cop[15] the poet relegates "all those who confuse the fortuitousness / Of art with something to be met with only / At extremity's brink." Instead, Tomlinson upholds humanity, not in spite of but because of its frailties, like the sufficient fragility in "Hill Walk." In similar fashion, the poet elsewhere has argued, "my poetry is aware of time as a necessary medium for such things [the chance meeting of Tomlinson and Paz at Rome airport] and it's also aware of the flux of time though it pleads that there *are* human fidelities that survive mere flux and that they *need* the passage of time to become what they are."[16] "The flux of time" is the necessary condition for both his poetry of recovery and what that poetry seeks to achieve – the active perceiving self's grasp of the true nature of things.

Consequently, in "The Chances of Rhyme," he concludes:

> To take chances, as to make rhymes
> Is human, but between chance and impenitence
>   (A half-rhyme) come dance, vigilance
> And circumstance (meaning all that is there
>   Besides you, when you are there). And between
> Rest-in-peace and precipice,
>   Inertia and perversion, come the varieties
> Increase, lease, re-lease (in both
>   Senses); and immersion, conversion – of inert
> Mass, that is, into energies to combat confusion.
>   Let rhyme be my conclusion.

The manner is witty and accomplished, in the manner of an epilogue to a Shakespearean comedy, and itself illustrates vividly and convincingly the "binding" nature of rhyme. The Romantic extremes are firmly rejected in favour of the familiar Tomlinson preferences for "Increase, lease, re-lease" and the "conversion" not of a religious or didactic kind but of "Mass ... into energies." The poetry of recovery serves both to conserve experience and to "combat confusion." For Tomlinson, metamorphosis – in which the contours of an experience have been carefully charted and translated, and the essence made known – has always brought clarity, precision, and enlightenment to shape and order the teeming, chaotic nature of the world. He has taught us to see, to appreciate the world, and to achieve that rhyming relationship which his work celebrates and shows to be at the heart of knowing and being.

# Conclusion

Charles Tomlinson remains one of the most distinctively modernist and avant-garde of contemporary British poets, enriched by traditions outside the English and promoting American poetics and experimentation. His travels, actual and literary, have imprinted upon his work an internationalism in stark contrast to the more insular, parochial attitudes prevailing in much British poetry of the last thirty years. While others have also been aware of European and American developments, Tomlinson, perhaps more than any other contemporary British poet, has assimilated them to his own poetic ends. That assimilation has been responsible in large part for persistent British suspicion and unwillingness to grant him the same status and acceptance he has achieved elsewhere. Yet, despite his internationalism, Tomlinson is essentially traditional and conservative in character and spirit: his subjects are the traditional ones (man, nature, society, time, history, death) and his techniques, while markedly experimental, are employed for intrinsically conservative ends (to preserve the sense of time and achieve the necessary "return," to recover experiences, to uphold order). His concerns, style, and tone remain distinctively English: Wordsworth more than William Carlos Williams has proved relevant as both parallel and precursor.

Despite his persistent objection to the parochialism of Philip Larkin and the Movement poets, Tomlinson shares with Larkin the same rootedness in time and place and the same profound concern for the character of English social life. While admitting to "a townsman's eye" (*CP* 322), he has not for the most part moved into the distinctively Larkin territory of English urban society. Nevertheless, he has persistently criticized the thoughtless demolition of towns and the vulgarity of much of our modern taste, and, for all his preoccupation with aesthetics, he has never promoted an Art-for-Art's Sake or cut himself off from the business of living and writing about everyday life. His landscapes are varied, ranging from Stoke-on-Trent to Lerici, Arizona, New Mexico, and New York, with his Gloucestershire valley predominant, and are generally rural, less heavily populated, less ugly than Larkin's. Yet in their quality of air or light, their mental analogues, they are also no less moral in significance. That morality is founded upon the organic relationship between self and world, and requires a self-imposed, Wordsworthian detachment, prerequisite to objectivity, accuracy, and freedom from egotistic inflation and distortion. Such detachment serves both a phenomenological and a social purpose: it constitutes part of the discipline essential to his scrupulous attention to the processes of the self, of perception and of the turning world; it bears also upon that acknowledgment of the otherness of things, whether people or world, which is central to civility and true relationship.

Tomlinson's virtues, as Donald Davie argued at the outset of the poet's career, are intrinsically Augustan: classical in their insistence upon moderation, restraint, austerity of outlook; impersonal in their objectivity and detachment; yet often witty and ironic in tone; always intelligent and rational, appealing to intellect and to common sense. Yet it is Wordsworth rather than Alexander Pope whom he more closely resembles, whether in his inclination to contemplation, his meditative tone, his preoccupation with memory, or his fondness for Wordsworthian subjects like the building of a wall or the rootedness of things. He shares Wordsworth's detachment and disinclination to alter a situation, his recognition of the need for contact while remaining respectful of the individuality of others, even at times a Wordsworthian speaking voice.

That measured voice lacks the deliberately shocking vulgarity of a Larkin or the dynamic physicality of a Ted Hughes, vital and effective as those qualities may be: Tomlinson's work may thus appear in comparison more academic, even élitist, less sympathetic of human frailty, less aware of contemporary horror. Such criticism, as we have seen, is misplaced and depends to no small extent upon the distinctively visual character of Tomlinson's work. His may be a painter's eye, acutely sensitive to the particulars of a landscape and to the negotiations in perception between self and world. Yet he is preoccupied with aesthetics and phenomenology because he is concerned with how we might see more precisely and completely and how we might live full, civilized lives.

Tomlinson has always been conscious of the dangers of Romanticism, but he has inherited the fundamental Romantic principle that wholeness of perception depends upon wholeness of self. Clarity and wholeness of perception are sought, therefore, because they in turn demand a similarly clear and whole self, free of extremism, excess, and apocalyptic tendencies, and possessed of balance, proportion, discrimination, and measure. Such qualities relate also to his religious vision, bringing intimations of Eden within time. His distinctive affirmations convince because they reveal intelligence, keenness, and control. But they move and illuminate because they celebrate, rather than simply record, the dynamic exchange between the creative self and the physical world; they offer fulfilment through accommodation with time and acknowledgment of both human worth and human frailty. Tomlinson shares with other contemporaries, British, European, and American, a common concern to construct the self; to enable man to come to terms with finiteness and death; and to provide that heightened awareness which makes the poet an essential figure in man's progress towards understanding and experience of the real. The distinctive articulation of that concern in a substantial body of work of the first order is the measure of his poetic achievement.

# Notes

INTRODUCTION

1 "Context," *London Magazine* ns 1 (Feb. 1962): 27.

2 Quoted by George Steiner, *Language and Silence: Essays 1958–1966* (London: Faber 1967), 72.

3 Claude Roy, Foreword, in Octavio Paz, Jacques Roubaud, Edoardo Sanguineti, and Charles Tomlinson, *Renga: A Chain of Poems*, 14. John Press likewise found the fact "significant, and to an Englishman depressing, that, like Robert Frost in his day, the poet Charles Tomlinson, scarcely granted a hearing in his own country, should have achieved success and the publication of his first substantial volume on the far side of the Atlantic." *Rule and Energy: Trends in British Poetry since the Second World War* (London: Oxford University Press 1963), 3. Tomlinson in a poem to Donald Davie aligned himself with Shelley and Lawrence as "exiles who had in common / Love for an island slow to learn of it / Or to return that love" (*CP* 342).

4 Calvin Bedient, *Eight Contemporary Poets: Charles Tomlinson, Donald Davie, R.S. Thomas, Philip Larkin, Ted Hughes, Thomas Kinsella, Stevie Smith, W.S. Graham* (London: Oxford University Press 1974), 1.

5 *Thomas Hardy and British Poetry* (London: Routledge and Kegan Paul 1973), 2. Cf. his review of *Seeing Is Believing* (April 1959), rept. Donald Davie, *The Poet in the Imaginary Museum – Essays of Two Decades*, ed. Barry Alpert (Manchester: Carcanet 1977), 66–71. Davie continued to berate Tomlinson's lack of recognition in Britain, in "Some Shires Revisited (4) Staffordshire," *In the Stopping Train* (Manchester: Carcanet 1977), 47. Michael Schmidt argued similarly, that "[Tomlinson's] work

has not had its due in England, though it has abroad. He merits more readers." "Charles Tomlinson at 50: A Celebration," *PN Review* 5 (1977): 33.

6 For Tomlinson's bad relations with the Movement, see his savagely satirical verse, "In the Movement," not republished, *New Statesman*, 22 Oct. 1955; and his unfavourable review of *New Lines*, ed. Robert Conquest, "The Middlebrow Muse," *EIC* 7 (April 1957): 208–17. For the subsequent controversy in *EIC*, see Donald Davie and D.J. Enright (July 1957): 343–5; Tomlinson and Ronald Gaskell (Oct. 1957): 460–2; Ronald Hayman and F.W. Bateson (Oct. 1957): 465–70; and Robert Conquest, 8 (April 1958): 225–7. Attacks and counter-attacks continued elsewhere for several years. For example, in Ian Hamilton, "Four Conversations," *London Magazine* 4 (Nov. 1964): 64–85, Thom Gunn doubted Tomlinson's originality and individuality, Larkin dismissed foreign poetry, while Tomlinson described the Movement as symptomatic of the suffocation of English art since Byron's death and blasted English criticism for its provincialism.

7 A. Alvarez and Donald Davie, "A Discussion," *the Review* 1 (April–May 1961): 17; rept. as "A New Aestheticism?" in *The Modern Poet: Essays from 'the Review,'* ed. Ian Hamilton (London: Macdonald 1968), 157–76. Cf. Colin Falck, in *Modern Poet*, ed. Hamilton, 14: "there is a deadening absence of other people in these poems most of the time" (1962).

8 Eric Homberger, "New Bearings," *Guardian*, 14 Nov. 1974, 16. Cf. his comment on Tomlinson in *The Art of the Real: Poetry in England and America since 1939* (London: Dent 1977), 102–6.

9 Charles Tomlinson, "Charles Tomlinson in Conversation," *PN Review* 5 (1977): 37.

10 Quoted by Ruth A. Grogan, "Charles Tomlinson: The Way of His World," *Contemporary Literature* 19 (Autumn 1978): 472.

11 *Contemporary Poets of the English Language*, ed. Rosalie Murphy (London: St James Press 1970), 1097.

12 *The Poet Speaks: Interviews with Contemporary Poets*, ed. Peter Orr (London: Routledge and Kegan Paul 1966), 252.

13 Elizabeth Jennings reviewed *Seeing Is Believing*, *London Magazine* 7 (Oct. 1960); Philip Hobsbaum, "The Growth of English Modernism," *Wisconsin Studies in Contemporary Literature* 6 (Winter–Spring 1965): 104.

14 Introducing *The Return*, a PBS Recommendation, *Poetry Book Society Bulletin*, Autumn 1987.

15 Introducing *The Shaft*, a PBS Recommendation, *Poetry Book Society Bulletin*, Spring 1978.

16 *Contemporary Poets of the English Language*, ed. Murphy, 1097.

CHAPTER ONE

1 To Hamilton, "Four Conversations," 83, Tomlinson admitted writing "unpublished Blake-Whitman 'prophetic books,' written and illustrated in '49 [which] had the grain of something new but they were technically wretched." As is true of many of the early influences upon Tomlinson, little remains after the earliest work to indicate the lasting effect of Blake's influence.

2 To Jed Rasula and Mike Erwin, "An Interview with Charles Tomlinson," *Contemporary Literature* 16 (Autumn 1975): 416, Tomlinson acknowledged the crucial contribution to his thought of Maurice Merleau-Ponty's *The Primacy of Perception*, a work he came upon by chance. Chance itself is a persistent late preoccupation: his chance encounter with Merleau-Ponty's work – *The Primacy of Perception, and Other Essays on Phenomenological Psychology, the Philosophy of Art, History and Politics*, ed. James M. Edie (Evanston: Northwestern University Press 1964) – roughly coincided in time with his encounter with the decalcomania of Oscar Domínguez (see below, chapter 5), a technique in which chance is central. Nevertheless, Tomlinson has always been concerned with the phenomenology of perception; he found much to his satisfaction also in John Berger's *Ways of Seeing* (New York: Viking 1973); and the influence upon him of both Merleau-Ponty and Berger can be exaggerated.

3 Rasula and Erwin, "Interview with Charles Tomlinson," 408, 416. The "meeting of person and presence" was misprinted as "melting," hence Tomlinson's poem "Misprint" (*CP* 302).

4 *Solo for a Glass Harmonica, Poems in Folio* I, no. 7 (San Francisco 1957).

5 Hamilton, "Four Conversations," 83.

6 Hopkins's influence is not especially evident after the earliest volume, *Relations and Contraries, Poems in Pamphlet* IX (Aldington, Kent: Hand and Flower Press 1951), although Tomlinson maintains Hopkins's concern with inscape and instress and shares his eye for the particular. One feels he might find Hopkins's Journal more valuable than his poetry, for much the same reason that he admires another Victorian, Ruskin – because both writers teach one how to see, particularly the natural world.

7 For "rotund emotions," see "Esthetique du Mal," xv, *Collected Poems of Wallace Stevens* (New York: Knopf 1964), 325. Cf. "A Primitive Like an Orb" (440–3) with its "giant," its "gorging good," its "central poem" celebrated as "The fulfillment of fulfillments, in opulent, / Last terms, the largest, bulging still with more."

8 Tomlinson told Rasula and Erwin, "Interview with Charles Tomlinson," 407, that the dryad passage referred to Büber's section, "I consider a tree," in *I and Thou.* Cf. *Eden* 11: "a dryad would only be a veil between yourself and a tree once your eyes had been opened by this other intenser nakedness" [when "confronted ... with a sense of the primal and the elemental" in the English Midlands landscape].

9 Rasula and Erwin, "Interview with Charles Tomlinson," 406.

10 Cf. Bedient, *Eight Contemporary Poets,* 2. Davie asked in 1977: "Could it be that Wordsworth's is the voice from our past that nowadays most needs to be attended to, though in fact it goes for the most part unheard?" *Poet in the Imaginary Museum,* ed. Alpert, 212.

11 *Poetry Book Society Bulletin,* Spring 1978. Cf. "For Danton" (*CP* 278–9), which takes its epigraph from *The Prelude,* and "Below Tintern" (292), another obvious acknowledgment.

12 Such a union of sense defining beauty Tomlinson found in William Carlos Williams. Charles Tomlinson, "Dr. Williams' Practice," *Encounter* 29 (Nov. 1967): 69.

13 The source for the frontier image is surely W.H. Auden: Brian John, "The Poetry of Charles Tomlinson," *Far Point* 3 (Fall-Winter 1969): 56. Grogan, "Charles Tomlinson: The Way of His World," 474, lists usefully "the following cluster of words: striation, channels, skeins, strands, lanes, filaments, ripples, currents, grains, veins, tracery, interlacing, unravelings, meshes, crosshatching, openwork, honeycombs, and networks." The list complements my own, of marriage, wedding, truce, frontier, bridge, thread, map.

14 See "The Ecstasy." Donne was another early influence, as evidenced in the Metaphysical love poems in *Relations and Contraries.* Although Tomlinson's subsequent work shows few obvious debts to him – the distinctively Metaphysical image of the eyebeam appears in his later work (e.g. "Rhymes," *CP* 290) together with the circle in *The Return* (see below, chapter 5) – Donne appears to haunt Tomlinson (*Renga* 36; cf. sonnet III$_7$).

15 Paul Mariani, "Tomlinson's Use of the Williams Triad," *Contemporary Literature* 18 (Summer 1977): 412, tells of Tomlinson's correspondence

with Williams, begun at Hugh Kenner's suggestion, in December 1957. Mariani rightly points out the importance of the three-ply line in capturing cadences of speech, a technique which works equally well for Tomlinson's English as for Williams's American speech. But he fails to note that the cadence is also visual and intellectual, capturing the rhythms of a perception, and that his own rearranging of Tomlinson's tercets with Marvellian couplets loses the sense of space which the three-ply line creates.

16 Rasula and Erwin, "Interview with Charles Tomlinson," 412, 406.

17 Tomlinson to Peter Orr (1961), *Poet Speaks*, ed. Orr, 250. Cf. Roy, who describes Tomlinson as numbering "Ruskin among his masters" (*Renga* 14). The debt is acknowledged in particular poems like "Frondes Agrestes" (*CP* 35) and in frequent references to the Victorian. Tomlinson has seen Ruskin's relevance to his own concern with rhyme, tracery, and the thread of experience. In a review, "Experience into Music: The Poetry of Basil Bunting," *Agenda* 4 (undated [Feb.-March 1966?]): 16, Tomlinson quotes Ruskin on Jean de Meung, author of the second part of the medieval French masterpiece, the *Roman de la Rose*: "There is to be rich rhyming and chiming, no matter how simply got, so only that the words jingle and tingle together with due art of interlacing and answering in different parts of the stanza, correspondent to the involutions of tracery and illumination."

18 This and subsequent quotations are from Tomlinson, " 'Not in Sequence of a Metronome,' " *Agenda: Special Issue on Rhythm* 10–11 (Autumn-Winter 1972-3): 53–4. The issue includes Stephen Srawley, "A Note on Musical and Poetic Rhythm," 114–18, commenting upon the problems he faced in setting Tomlinson's "Da Capo" to music, and publishing his score (119–20). Srawley has also written the score for a sequence of Tomlinson's Eden poems.

19 Wallace Stevens, "Three Academic Pieces," *The Necessary Angel: Essays on Reality and the Imagination* (New York: Vintage 1965), 78, 77.

20 Rasula and Erwin, "Interview with Charles Tomlinson," 412. Cf. Georgia O'Keeffe, another of Tomlinson's American sources: "One morning the world was covered with snow. As I walked past the V of the red hills, I was startled to see them white. It was a beautiful early morning – black crows flying over the white. It became another painting – the now-covered hills holding up the sky, a black bird flying, always there, always going away": *Georgia O'Keeffe* (New York: Viking 1976), pl. 86, "A Black Bird with Snow-Covered Red Hills."

21 Cf. W.B. Yeats, "Cuchulain's Fight with the Sea," line 86, in which Cuchulain fights "with the invulnerable tide."

22 Writing of the necessary conjunction of poetry and music, Tomlinson has argued: "From Schoenberg and even more so from Webern, our awareness of the value of the single note and its concomitant silence has brought about a parallel extension to that which American poetry offers us. I further believe that the poet must consciously try to make up on his own behalf for the great divorce which has come about between poetry and music." *Poetry Book Society Bulletin*, June 1963.

23 *Poet Speaks*, ed. Orr, 250–1.

24 *Poet Speaks*, ed. Orr, 252. Cf. Tomlinson's rejection of Thomas in "Antecedents, III. Lacunae," lines 29–31, *CP* 52. Donald Davie, *Purity of Diction in English Verse* (1952; rept. with postscript, London: Routledge and Kegan Paul 1967), 198–9, in his 1966 Postscript, writes of such rejection of Thomas and of "all the values of Bohemia" both by Tomlinson and by the Movement poets generally.

25 Introducing *The Return*, *Poetry Book Society Bulletin*, Autumn 1987.

26 *The Letters of John Keats, 1814–1821*, ed. Hyder Edward Rollins (Cambridge, Mass.: Harvard University Press 1958), 2:167.

27 On several occasions Tomlinson has associated stone or house with patience: *CP* 40–2, 70–2, 121–2, 206–7, *Versions* 10. In "The Flood," however, he concedes: "It was the night of the flood first took away / My trust in stone" (*CP* 346). Nevertheless, a house, particularly the poet's own eighteenth-century Gloucestershire cottage, persistently images a rootedness in which meaning can be found and time withstood. Both *The Flood* and *Airborn* particularly evidence the centrality of "house."


CHAPTER TWO


1 The "neither-nor" distinction is used frequently in the early work (*CP* 5, 7, 28, 37) and is bolstered further by other negatives (unfit, ignored, unlike, untaught, unalterable, unfelt). Defining what things are not (as in stanza 4 "On the Hall at Stowey," 40) is an essential stage in Tomlinson's process towards knowledge.

2 Rasula and Erwin, "Interview with Charles Tomlinson," 415.

3 *Poetry Book Society Bulletin*, Autumn 1974. The volume was the Autumn choice. Both place and return are equally central to *The Flood*, to *Notes from New York*, and to Tomlinson's most recent volume, *The*

*Return*, where, despite his persistent internationalism, he shows that all roads lead back to Gloucestershire and England.

4 Michael Edwards, "Charles Tomlinson: Notes on Tradition and Impersonality," *CQ* 15 (Summer 1973): 139. Monroe K. Spears, "Shapes and Surfaces: David Jones, with a Glance at Charles Tomlinson," *Contemporary Literature* 12 (Fall 1971): 418–19, notes the parallel with D.H. Lawrence.

5 *Poetry Book Society Bulletin*, June 1963.

6 Charles Tomlinson, in "The State of Poetry – A Symposium," *the Review: Tenth Anniversary Issue*, 29–30 (Spring-Summer 1972): 50–1.

7 *Poetry Book Society Bulletin*, Spring 1978. The volume was the Spring recommendation.

8 Cf. William Blake, "Where man is not nature is barren": *Marriage of Heaven and Hell*, 10:68, in *The Poetry and Prose of William Blake*, ed. David V. Erdman (New York: Doubleday 1965), 37. Cf. Wallace Stevens, "Anecdote of the Jar," "The Idea of Order at Key West," although his entire work, poetry and prose, centres on the primacy of the imagination in its ability to shape the temporal flux of nature. Tomlinson's "The Hill (*CP* 114) is a curious fusion of both those Stevens poems. That nature can and should.be "improved" is also, however, an Augustan dictum (see Alexander Pope, "Moral Essays, Epistle IV: To Richard Boyle, Earl of Burlington," lines 47–70), a parallel which, given Tomlinson's Augustanism, is as relevant as those of Blake and Stevens.

9 See *BW*, plates 1–4, 31, 49.

10 Ruth A. Grogan, "Charles Tomlinson: Poet as Painter," *CQ* 19 (Winter 1977): 74, makes a similar point. Thomas H. Getz distinguishes Tomlinson from both O'Keeffe and D.H. Lawrence, seeing him as feeling overwhelmed by the American desert: "Charles Tomlinson's Manscapes," *Modern Poetry Studies* 11 (1983): 210. What is not debatable, however, is how much Tomlinson has been attracted to O'Keeffe's vision of the New Mexican landscape and how he has described that vision in his own distinctive terms (*Some Americans* 77).

11 *Solo for a Glass Harmonica*, unpaginated.

12 Blake, "The Ghost of Abel," *Poetry and Prose of William Blake*, ed. Erdman, 268: "Nature has no outline: but the Imagination has. Nature has no Tune: but Imagination has!"

13 Immanuel Kant defined his concept of an "ethical commonwealth" as "a church": "The visible church is the actual union of men into a whole which harmonizes with that ideal." *Religion within the Limits of Reason*

*Alone*, trans. with intro. Theodore M. Greene and Hoyt H. Hudson (New York: Harper and Row 1960), 92.

14 Tomlinson, in "The State of Poetry – A Symposium," 50, declared sharply: "there are certain things one would like to see an end of: the invitation to prolonged adolescence from Liverpool; the suicide mania (already fading, perhaps, now that radio, television and the Sunday press have worn it out); Francis Bacon-like screamings about the absurdity of the universe; the 'Look, I'm ruining my life' type of poetry (Requiescat in pace, John Berryman)." Extremism has resulted in "the breakdown ... of relations with the world of Wordsworth (by 'world' I mean that essential 'thinking into the human heart' which, allied with the insights of the phenomenologists, might have given us back a human universe)." More recently, in "Instead of an Essay" (*CP* 342), he dismissed the passing "fashions" of "the buddha, shamanism, suicide."

CHAPTER THREE

1 The address was the annual Phi Beta Kappa convocation address delivered by Tomlinson as distinguished visiting professor at Colgate. Because *The Poem as Initiation* (Hamilton, NY: Colgate University Press 1968) is unpaginated, I am unable to provide references to quotations from the address. Since "Swimming Chenango Lake" appeared subsequently in *The Way of a World*, I provide page references from *CP*. "Chenango Lake" is Tomlinson's own renaming of Poolville Pond, New York.

2 Tomlinson's first poems, *Relations and Contraries*, reveal the influence of Yeats but, like that of Hopkins and Donne, it is soon absorbed or overcome; indeed, Yeats is dismissed later for excessive mythologizing (*CP* 71). Nevertheless, in "Yeats and the Practising Poet," *An Honoured Guest: New Essays on W.B. Yeats*, ed. Denis Donoghue and J.R. Mulryne (New York: St Martin's Press 1966), 1–7, Tomlinson writes appreciatively of Yeats's worth and, while admitting to having imitated him earlier, advises against such imitation.

3 Grogan, "Charles Tomlinson: The Way of His World," 479, has argued that "In the post-1969 work the word 'grasp' joins 'see' in importance," a development she traces to the influence primarily of Merleau-Ponty, although she points also to William Carlos Williams and other American poets and painters (480–3). While she may be right to stress the increased kinetic quality of Tomlinson's perceptions after 1969 and his excited

reading of Merleau-Ponty, such a quality was already present in earlier poems (e.g., "Paring the Apple" and "At Holwell Farm"). Indeed, "grasp," which is used in the latter poem and elsewhere in the early work (*CP* 17, 103), is not an exclusively late term in Tomlinson's vocabulary; it disappears from *The Flood* (1981) where it is replaced by the more Lawrencean "touch" (317, 319). In *NNY* (1984) both terms coexist (*NNY* 19, 41, 45, 48) and the hand is particularly prominent (13, 41, 54, 60).

4  Tomlinson's poetry contains numerous examples of particular moments – "instances," as the third section of *The Way of a World* describes them; what, with characteristic emphasis upon the temporal flux, he called previously "the flowing instant" (*CP* 151). Increasingly in the later work such moments acquire a numinous quality, imaged as Eden or, more recently, perfection.

5  In its insistence upon autumnal climax and perpetual flux, imaged by the rippling water, the conclusion is reminiscent of the final lines of Stevens's "Sunday Morning": "And, in the isolation of the sky, / At evening, casual flocks of pigeons make / Ambiguous undulations as they sink / Downward to darkness, on extended wings" (*Collected Poems of Wallace Stevens*, 70). A similarly Stevensian circling descent into darkness is present in *The Flood* (*CP* 319, 320, 338).

6  Lawrence's influence upon Tomlinson has been considerable. His Visiting Professorship at the University of New Mexico in 1961 was financed by a D.H. Lawrence Fellowship, and in his New Mexico poems he is very much aware of Lawrence's presence. "Anecdote" (*CP* 171) was written at Lawrence's Kiowa Ranch, while in his *America West South West* preface Tomlinson quotes Lawrence approvingly. He shares not only Lawrence's fascination with the American South-West and its people but also his emphasis upon touch and sense of place, and, not the least, his English-ness and Midlands origins. While Henry Gifford applied Lawrence's terms to Tyutchev – "the unrestful, ungraspable poetry of the sheer present" (*Versions* 4) – the terms are equally applicable to Tomlinson. Cf. Michael Kirkham, "Negotiations," *EIC* 17 (July 1967): 367–74. The New Mexican landscape, however, is rich in associations with Georgia O'Keeffe also (see ch. 2, n. 10): her paintings provided Tomlinson with his "first glimpse" of that landscape (*Some Americans* 77); in 1929 she painted at Kiowa Ranch and met Lawrence's friends, Tony and Mabel Dodge Luhan (see Jan Garden Castro, *The Art and Life of Georgia O'Keeffe* [New York: Crown 1985], 79ff.); while Tomlinson's chapter on O'Keeffe in *Some Americans* describes his 1963 visit to her adobe house in Abiquiu.

7 Charles Tomlinson/Alan Ross, "Words and Water: Charles Tomlinson and His Poetry," *London Magazine*, Jan. 1981, 34.

8 Tomlinson, reviewing Davie's *Ezra Pound: Poet as Sculptor, Agenda* 4 (Oct.-Nov. 1965): 46–9.

9 This and subsequent quotations are from Tomlinson, "Middlebrow Muse," 208–17.

10 "If it were not for the Poetic or Prophetic character the Philosophic & Experimental would soon be at the ratio of all things, & stand still unable to do other than repeat the same dull round over again." *There Is No Natural Religion*, in *Poetry and Prose of William Blake*, ed. Erdman, 1.

11 "Auguries of Innocence," *Poetry and Prose of William Blake*, ed. Erdman, 481. Cf. D.H. Lawrence, "Why the Novel Matters," *Phoenix: The Posthumous Papers of D.H. Lawrence (1936)*, ed. Edward D. McDonald (New York: Viking 1968), 533–4: "If you're a novelist, you know that paradise is in the palm of your hand, and on the end of your nose, because both are alive."

12 Quoted by Tomlinson, *Some Americans* 90. As Tomlinson notes, O'Keeffe's source lay in "Arthur Wesley Dow, whose book *Composition* and whose teaching methods introduced the ideas of Fenellosa into American art schools" (90). Through Alan Bement at the University of Virginia she likewise learned "the idea that music could be translated into something for the eye" (*Georgia O'Keeffe*, pl. 14: "Music – Pink and Blue I") and in turn has described her shell and shingle paintings as "singing shapes" (pl. 51).

CHAPTER FOUR

1 Cf. Seamus Heaney, "Envies and Identifications: Dante and the Modern Poet," *Irish University Review* 15 (Spring 1985): 5–19, where Heaney writes of this very process. Cf. also Heaney's use of the ancient Irish poet-king, Sweeney, in his translation of the early Irish poem, *Sweeney Astray* (Derry: Field Day 1983) and in his own volume *Station Island* (London: Faber 1984). Sweeney serves a function larger than mere persona: through his translation of Sweeney's poem, Heaney finds "himself through the original."

2 Rasula and Erwin, "Interview with Charles Tomlinson," 406–7.

3 Introduction to César Vallejo, *Ten Versions from "Trilce,"* trans. Charles Tomlinson and Henry Gifford (Cerrillos, New Mexico: San Marcos Press 1970), 8.

4 By Stephen Srawley; see above ch. 1, n. 18.

5 While the poem suggests its origins in actual experience, one source, as indicated in the poem's epigraph, is clearly Jean-Paul Sartre. The situation also parallels a passage from Kafka to which Tomlinson has himself referred: "To begin ... and with that constant longing, perhaps, of the young man in Kafka's story, 'to catch a glimpse of things as they may have been before they show themselves to me' " (*BW* 20). In any case, the statement, as Octavio Paz points out, "defines [Tomlinson's] own purpose admirably" (8).

CHAPTER FIVE

1 *Poetry Book Society Bulletin*, June 1963.

2 "Four Conversations," 84–5.

3 Rasula and Erwin, "Interview with Charles Tomlinson," 414–15.

4 Tomlinson, "Introduction: Marianne Moore, Her Poetry and Her Critics," *Marianne Moore: A Collection of Critical Essays*, ed. Charles Tomlinson (Englewood Cliffs, NJ: Prentice-Hall 1969), 9. Cf. his fine tribute, "Letter to Dr. Williams" (1957), rept. *William Carlos Williams: A Critical Anthology*, ed. Charles Tomlinson (Harmondsworth: Penguin 1972), 364–5: in England, Tomlinson writes, "they are deaf to everything / except the quatrain / which is virtually / as useless as the couplet." Cf. "Remembering Williams" (*CP* 228) and his poetic tributes to Marianne Moore, "Ship's Waiters" and "Over Brooklyn Bridge" (100, 101–2).

5 Tomlinson, "Last of Lands," review, *New Statesman*, 28 April 1961, 674.

6 *Poetry Book Society Bulletin*, June 1963.

7 Charles Tomlinson, Introduction, *William Carlos Williams: A Critical Anthology*, ed. Tomlinson, 37.

8 *William Carlos Williams: A Critical Anthology*, ed. Tomlinson, 364–5.

9 Letter dated Sept. or Oct. 1861, *Mark Twain's Letters*, arr. Albert Bigelow Paine (New York: Harper 1917), 1:54–5. Tomlinson gave the same treatment to a letter to him from George Oppen; see Rasula and Erwin, "Interview with Charles Tomlinson," 414. Cf. his use of nineteenth-century accounts of a beached whale in the Severn estuary in "The Littleton Whale" (*CP* 343–6), a poem dedicated to the memory of Charles Olson and indebted to him.

10 "Charles Tomlinson in Conversation," *PN Review* 5 (1977): 37.

11 "I describe the demolition of parts of Bristol – humble and rather fine streets in their unpretentious way, neighbourhoods never to be restored. I

catch sight of an oldish couple dragging away scrap iron, old magazines, odds and ends in a battered perambulator and this I suppose is a use of myth, though I dislike the word 'use.' It's a use of myth in so far as I see them as Adam and Eve long-banished from Eden, but I wouldn't want to expand the thing to Wagnerian proportion." Rasula and Erwin, "Interview with Charles Tomlinson," 407.

12 *Poetry Book Society Bulletin*, Autumn 1974.

13 Rasula and Erwin, "Interview with Charles Tomlinson," 410. Cf. Tomlinson/Ross, "Words and Water: Charles Tomlinson and His Poetry," 39. Davie has argued that Tomlinson's "quarrel with [his] contemporaries is in part a political quarrel, or at least ... has immediate political implications," and he points to Tomlinson's sympathy with Yeats's "*élitist* and hierarchical politics." *Hardy and British Poetry*, 76.

14 Rasula and Erwin, "Interview with Charles Tomlinson," 409.

15 Crewe because it is synonymous in British vernacular with the ugly, undesirable, and abandoned; Mow Cop perhaps because the Staffordshire town is known for its eighteenth-century folly, perhaps because it was "the birthplace of Primitive Methodism": see John Wain, *Sprightly Running: Part of an Autobiography* (New York: St Martin's Press 1963), 146.

16 Rasula and Erwin, "Interview with Charles Tomlinson," 409.

# Bibliography

PRIMARY TEXTS

*Poetry*

Tomlinson, Charles. *Relations and Contraries. Poems in Pamphlet* IX. Aldington: Hand and Flower Press 1951.
– *The Necklace*. Swinford, Eynsham: Fantasy Press 1955; reissued with intro. Donald Davie. London: Oxford University Press 1966.
– "In the Movement." *New Statesman*, 22 Oct. 1955.
– *Solo for a Glass Harmonica. Poems in Folio* I, no. 7. San Francisco 1957.
– *Seeing Is Believing*. New York: Oxford University Press 1958; London: Oxford University Press 1960.
– *A Peopled Landscape*. London: Oxford University Press 1963.
– *American Scenes*. London: Oxford University Press 1966.
– *The Way of a World*. London: Oxford University Press 1969.
– *America West South West*. np.: San Marco Press 1970.
– with Octavio Paz, Jacques Roubaud, and Edoardo Sanguineti. *Renga: A Chain of Poems*. Foreword Claude Roy. New York: Braziller 1971.
– *Written on Water*. London: Oxford University Press 1972.
– *The Way In*. London: Oxford University Press 1974.
– *The Shaft*. Oxford: Oxford University Press 1978.
– *The Flood*. Oxford: Oxford University Press 1981.
– with Octavio Paz. *Airborn/Hijos del Aire*. London: Anvil Press Poetry 1981.
– *Notes from New York*. Oxford: Oxford University Press 1984.
– *Collected Poems*. Oxford: Oxford University Press 1985.

- "The Miracle of the Bottle and the Fishes." *With a Poet's Eye: A Tate Gallery Anthology*. Ed. Pat Adams. London: Tate Gallery 1986.
- *The Return*. Oxford: Oxford University Press 1987.

### Graphics

Tomlinson, Charles. *Words and Images*. Covent Garden Poetry, no. 1. Ed. Ronald Hayman. London: Covent Garden Press 1972.
- *In Black and White: The Graphics of Charles Tomlinson*. Intro. Octavio Paz. Cheadle: Carcanet 1976.
- *Eden: Graphics and Poetry*. Bristol: Redcliffe Poetry 1986.

### Translations

Tomlinson, Charles. With Henry Gifford. *Versions from Fyodor Tyutchev, 1803–1873*. Intro. Henry Gifford. London: Oxford University Press 1960.
- With Henry Gifford. *Castilian Ilexes: Versions from Antonio Machado, 1875–1939*. Intro. Henry Gifford. London: Oxford University Press 1963.
- with Henry Gifford. *Ten Versions from "Trilce" by César Vallejo*. Cerillos, New Mexico: San Marcos Press 1970.
- ed. *The Oxford Book of Verse in English Translation*. Oxford: Oxford University Press 1980.
- *Translations*. Oxford: Oxford University Press 1983.

### Criticism

Tomlinson, Charles. "The Middlebrow Muse." Review of *New Lines*, ed. Robert Conquest. *Essays in Criticism* 7 (April 1957): 208–17; and response in "The Critical Forum" (Oct. 1957): 460.
- "Last of Lands." *New Statesman*, 28 April 1961, 674.
- *Poetry Book Society Bulletin*, June 1963. Note on *A Peopled Landscape*.
- guest ed. *the Review: Black Mountain issue* 10 (Jan. 1964).
- guest ed. *Agenda: special Louis Zukovsky issue* 3 (Dec. 1964).
- *Agenda* 4 (Oct.-Nov. 1965): 46–9. Review of Donald Davie, *Ezra Pound: Poet as Sculptor*.
- "Experience into Music: The Poetry of Basil Bunting." Review, *Agenda* 4 (Feb.-March 1966): 11–17.
- "Yeats and the Practising Poet." *An Honoured Guest: New Essays on W.B. Yeats*, ed. Denis Donoghue and J.R. Mulryne, 1–7. New York: St Martin's Press 1966.

- "Dr. Williams' Practice." *Encounter* 29 (Nov. 1967): 69.
- *The Poem as Initiation*. Hamilton, NY: Colgate University Press 1968.
- ed. *Marianne Moore: A Collection of Critical Essays*. Englewood Cliffs, NJ: Prentice-Hall 1969.
- "The State of Poetry – A Symposium." *the Review: Tenth Anniversary Issue* 29–30 (Spring-Summer 1972): 48–51.
- ed. *William Carlos Williams: A Critical Anthology*. Harmondsworth: Penguin 1972.
- " 'Not in Sequence of a Metronome.' " *Agenda: Special Issue on Rhythm* 10–11 (Autumn-Winter 1972–73): 53–4.
- *Poetry Book Society Bulletin*, Autumn 1974. Note on *The Way In*.
- *Poetry Book Society Bulletin*, Spring 1978. Note on *The Shaft*.
- *Some Americans: A Personal Record*. Berkeley: University of California Press 1981.
- *Poetry and Metamorphosis*. Cambridge: Cambridge University Press 1983.
- *Poetry Book Society Bulletin*, Autumn 1987. Note on *The Return*.

*Interviews*

Hamilton, Ian. "Four Conversations." *London Magazine* 4 (Nov. 1964): 82–5.
*The Poet Speaks: Interviews with Contemporary Poets*. Ed. Peter Orr, 250–5. London: Routledge and Kegan Paul 1966.
Rasula, Jed, and Mike Erwin. "An Interview with Charles Tomlinson." *Contemporary Literature* 16 (Autumn 1975): 405–16.
Schmidt, Michael. "Charles Tomlinson in Conversation." *PN Review* 5 (1977): 35–40.
Ross, Alan. "Words and Water: Charles Tomlinson and His Poetry." *London Magazine*, Jan. 1981, 23–39.

CRITICAL ESSAYS ON
CHARLES TOMLINSON

Alvarez, A. and Donald Davie. "A Discussion." *the Review* 1 (April-May 1961): 10–25; rept. as "A New Aestheticism?" in *The Modern Poet: Essays from 'the Review,'* ed. Ian Hamilton, 157–76. London: Macdonald 1968.
Bateson, F.W. "The Critical Forum." *Essays in Criticism* 7 (Oct. 1957): 468–70.
Bedient, Calvin. *Eight Contemporary Poets: Charles Tomlinson, Donald Davie, R.S. Thomas, Philip Larkin, Ted Hughes, Thomas Kinsella, Stevie Smith, W.S. Graham*. London: Oxford University Press 1974.

Conquest, Robert. "The Critical Forum." *Essays in Criticism* 8 (April 1958): 225-7.

Davie, Donald. *Purity of Diction in English Verse*. 1952; rept. with postscript, London: Routledge and Kegan Paul 1967.

– *Thomas Hardy and British Poetry*. London: Routledge and Kegan Paul 1973.

– *The Poet in the Imaginary Museum: Essays of Two Decades*. Ed. Barry Alpert. Manchester: Carcanet 1977.

– "The Critical Forum." *Essays in Criticism* 7 (July 1957): 343-4.

Edwards, Michael. "Charles Tomlinson: Notes on Tradition and Impersonality." *Critical Quarterly* 15 (Summer 1973): 133-44.

Enright, D.J. "The Critical Forum." *Essays in Criticism* 7 (July 1957): 344-5.

Falck, Colin. "Dreams and Responsibilities" (1962). In *The Modern Poet: Essays from 'the Review'*, ed. Ian Hamilton, 1-16. London: Macdonald 1968.

Gaskell, Ronald. "The Critical Forum." *Essays in Criticism* 7 (Oct. 1957): 461-2.

Getz, Thomas H. "Charles Tomlinson's Manscapes." *Modern Poetry Studies* 11 (1983).

Grogan, Ruth A. "Charles Tomlinson: Poet as Painter." *Critical Quarterly* 19 (Winter 1977): 71-7.

– "Charles Tomlinson: The Way of His World." *Contemporary Literature* 19 (Autumn 1978): 472-96.

Hobsbaum, Philip. "The Growth of English Modernism." *Wisconsin Studies in Contemporary Literature* 6 (Winter-Spring 1965): 97-105.

Homberger, Eric. *The Art of the Real: Poetry in England and America since 1939*. London: Dent 1977.

– "New Bearings." *Guardian*, 14 Nov. 1974, 16.

Jennings, Elizabeth. Review of *Seeing Is Believing*. *London Magazine* 7 (Oct. 1960).

John, Brian. "The Poetry of Charles Tomlinson." *Far Point* 3 (Fall-Winter 1969): 50-61.

Kirkham, Michael. "Negotiations." Review of *American Scenes*. *Essays in Criticism* 17 (July 1967): 367-74.

Mariani, Paul. "Tomlinson's Use of the Williams Triad." *Contemporary Literature* 18 (Summer 1977): 405-15.

Murphy, Rosalie, ed. *Contemporary Poets of the English Language*. London: St James Press 1970.

Press, John. *Rule and Energy: Trends in British Poetry since the Second World War*. London: Oxford University Press 1963.

Schmidt, Michael. "Charles Tomlinson at 50: A Celebration." *PN Review* 5 (1977): 33.

Spears, Monroe K. "Shapes and Surfaces: David Jones, with a glance at Charles Tomlinson." *Contemporary Literature* 12 (Fall 1971): 402–19.

Srawley, Stephen. "A Note on Musical and Poetic Rhythm." *Agenda: Special Issue on Rhythm*. 10–11 (Autumn-Winter 1972-3): 114–20.


OTHER WORKS CITED


Berger, John. *Ways of Seeing*. New York: Viking 1973.

Blake, William. *The Poetry and Prose of William Blake*. Ed. David V. Erdman. New York: Doubleday 1965.

Castro, Jan Garden. *The Art and Life of Georgia O'Keeffe*. New York: Crown 1985.

Davie, Donald. *In the Stopping Train*. Manchester: Carcanet 1977.

Graves, Robert. In "Context." *London Magazine*, ns 1 (Feb. 1962): 27.

Heaney, Seamus. "Envies and Identifications: Dante and the Modern Poet." *Irish University Review* 15 (Spring 1985): 5–19.

– *Sweeney Astray*. Derry: Field Day 1983.

– *Station Island*. London: Faber 1984.

Kant, Immanuel. *Religion within the Limits of Reason Alone*. Trans. with intro. Theodore M. Greene and Hoyt H. Hudson. New York: Harper and Row 1960.

Keats, John. *The Letters of John Keats, 1814–1821*. Ed. Hyder Edward Rollins. 2 vols. Cambridge, Mass.: Harvard University Press 1958.

Lawrence, D.H. *Phoenix: The Posthumous Papers*. Ed. Edward D. McDonald. New York: Viking 1968.

Merleau-Ponty, Maurice. *The Primacy of Perception, and Other Essays on Phenomenological Psychology, the Philosophy of Art, History and Politics*. Ed. James M. Edie. Evanston: Northwestern University Press 1964.

[O'Keeffe, Georgia.] *Georgia O'Keeffe*. New York: Viking 1976.

Steiner, George. *Language and Silence: Essays 1958–1966*. London: Faber 1967.

Stevens, Wallace. *Collected Poems*. New York: Knopf 1964.

– *The Necessary Angel: Essays on Reality and the Imagination*. New York: Vintage 1965.

Twain, Mark. *Mark Twain's Letters*. Arr. Albert Bigelow Paine. 2 vols. New York: Harper 1917.

Wain, John. *Sprightly Running: Part of an Autobiography*. New York: St Martin's Press 1963.

# Index